The
Organizer

The
Organizer

SECRETS AND SYSTEMS

FROM THE WORLD'S

TOP EXECUTIVE ASSISTANTS

Anna-Carin Jean

ReganBooks
An Imprint of HarperCollins*Publishers*

Illustrations by Jim Houghton

FIRST EDITION

Designed by Kris Tobiassen

Library of Congress Cataloging-in-Publication Data
Jean, Anna-Carin.
    The organizer : secrets and systems from the world's top executive assistants / Anna-Carin Jean.
       p.   cm.
   ISBN 0-06-039229-0
   1. Office practice—Handbooks, manuals, etc.   2. Office management—Handbooks, manuals, etc.   3. Secretaries.
I. Title
HF5547.5.J43   1999
651.3—dc21   98-43020
                                     CIP

98 99 00 01 02 ❖/RRD 10 9 8 7 6 5 4 3 2 1

Contents

Acknowledgments vii

Introduction ix

ONE Office Etiquette...1

TWO Telephones..9

THREE Mail 33

FOUR Filing 39

FIVE Computers..47

SIX Meetings and Scheduling 65

SEVEN Travel and Itineraries 77

EIGHT Temporary Assistance 93

NINE Interns 99

TEN Personal Errands and
Personal Assistants 111

ELEVEN Communication 121

TWELVE The Dress Code 133

THIRTEEN The Cheat Book 141

Closing Words 145

Index 147

Acknowledgments

This book would not have been possible without the help, encouragement, and patience of the following people:

Angelica Canales, Todd Silverstein, Jeremie Ruby-Strauss, and everyone at ReganBooks.

Rachael "BeBe" Lerner for hours of interviewing and writing for this project.

Jamie Caniffe, Sandy Pampel, and the boys at Division 1 Entertainment for their support and encouragement.

Amanda Ziskin and Dave Williams for their hard work in organizing interviews with executive assistants.

All of the executive assistants who lent their systems and organizational secrets to this book.

Judith Regan for giving me this opportunity.

Mom, Dad, Paul, Amy, and Michael for supporting me through all of the crazy jobs that I had which gave me the experience to write this book.

Anthony Fischli for being the voice of reason and for housing me while I finished the book.

Finally, thank you to Rob Hart, who pushed me to get the book published. Babe—now we can start counting chickens!

In Sweden we say,

Tusen Tack

It means a thousand thanks.

I wrote this book for and because of my good friend, Andrew Steinberg. In the short period that I worked for him, he challenged me and taught me to challenge myself more than anyone I have worked for. Because of him, I push myself and accept nothing less than the greatest success. For this, Andrew, I am eternally grateful.

Introduction

Do you remember the scene in *The Wizard of Oz* when Dorothy and her crew realize that one little man who hides behind a giant curtain runs all of Oz? The residents of Oz were happy along their yellow brick road and didn't care to know how it ran and why it ran smoothly. Executive assistants are a lot like the giant curtain. If they do their jobs properly, they make their bosses look great, business runs well, and no one on the outside really knows about the hard work that happens behind the scenes. Executive assistants organize their bosses' lives, schedule and prepare their meetings, set up their travel, and make sure that anything the boss will need to get the job done is prepared professionally and on time. A top-notch assistant can make a boss look as good as the Wizard.

Why would you want to be the person behind the boss? Opportunity—that's why. Unless you are very, very lucky (or born into it), you do not become the boss right away. Most executives have worked very hard for a long time to get the position they have now. The best way to move ahead is to learn from someone who is doing what you want to do. There is no better position to be in than this person's right hand—their executive assistant. You have access to *everything* they read, write, and say. You are involved in all aspects of their job—even more than their department heads because you witness every meeting, phone call, and fax from their inception to their completion. A smart, hardworking, and organized executive assistant can move ahead very fast in today's business world if they pay attention and do well as the person behind the boss.

This book is a workable, usable guide. Use it as you would use a road map. It will give you the basic tools to succeed as an assistant, but you need to take the tools and expand and build on them. Once you are comfortable with the basics, you should be able to create your own systems for organization based on what works for you. Like a map, this book can give you the direction and path to take, but you need to be the one to make the move.

I started off as an executive assistant. There were days when I loved it and other days when I hated it! But I stuck to it because I believed that I could move ahead. I was fortunate to have had terrific bosses. I owe so much of what I know, what I do now, and how I do things to the employers of my past. Every opportunity that has come my way was instigated by one of my former employers' recommendations of me—even this book.

If you have the opportunity to be an executive assistant for a good employer, take it. Work hard, absorb all the information you can, make your boss look good, and you will be on your way!

Good luck!

CHAPTER ONE

Office Etiquette

HERE IS A STORY FROM AN ASSISTANT NAMED DEBI:

I had recently started at a new firm. It was my second week, and I was still settling in. In my previous positions I had not needed to do personal things for my bosses or anyone else in the office. One day during lunch one of the partners of the firm came out of her office and shouted to no one in particular, "Can someone go out and pick up my lunch order?" I ignored her and went about my business. My co-workers were all looking at me. Evidently, because I was in her line of sight, the comment was directed at me. I was instructed to grab some petty cash and schlep down the street for her lunch. Upon my return, I escorted the brown paper lunch bag into her office. I noticed there was someone else in the office with her. I figured that he was her friend and they were just hanging out. I held out the bag to her and turned to walk away. She grabbed my arm and said through her teeth, "Can you put it on a plate?" I walked out of her office, went to the kitchen, found a plate, and put the styrofoam containers onto it. Right before I opened her door, her assistant caught me and said, "You need to take everything out of the containers and put them onto the plate. Make it look nice and not 'take-out-ish.' Remember to bring in a napkin and utensils." I went back to the kitchen, set out the meal as instructed, and walked back into her office. She snatched the plate from me and handed it to the man in the office. She growled through her teeth, "Thank you." I left her office, perplexed. My co-workers explained to me that when at the office, it's all about presentation. Also, the lunch was for the other person, possibly a client whom the boss wanted to impress. What better way to make a great impression than by having a top-notch staff at her fingertips that she can rely on for one hundred percent perfection?

While office etiquette is a topic broad enough to fill a book or two of its own, this chapter gives you the basics. Without good etiquette, no amount of accomplishment will overcome the lack of a professional image. The following tips are not hard to understand, and you will find that most of them are commonsense things such as being polite to clients and co-workers, being neat, admitting your mistakes, and helping out when others are swamped. This probably isn't new to you, but we all need a little reminder every once in a while!

CLIENTS AND BUSINESS ASSOCIATES

A client or associate is someone you are trying to impress. You want them to feel confident about their decision to bring their business to you. You are often the one who creates the first impression of your company when a client comes to visit. So, remember all of those manners that your mother taught you and use them. Be as friendly and polite as you can be. Never make the client feel like they are interrupting your busy work day.

- Introduce yourself to the client. Make eye contact as you shake their hand.
- When a client comes into the office, always offer them something to drink. If they ask for coffee, make sure to ask how they would like it. If they ask for Equal, do not grab Sweet'n Low and expect them not to notice. There is a difference.
- When a client comes into the building for a meeting, always escort them to the meeting area. You may be busy, but your boss will allow you a moment to personally escort the client rather then allow them to wander aimlessly through the building.
- The client should be waiting in a comfortable waiting area until your boss is ready for the meeting. Your boss may not like the client sitting in their office waiting for them.
- If you have to interrupt a meeting to give a message to someone in the meeting, excuse yourself for interrupting and be brief with your message.

CONFLICTS

- When you are angry, learn to walk away. Take a quick trot around the block. Do whatever it takes to calm down and think rationally before you return to your office.

- If you must have a confrontation, have all of the facts and speak in a calm, rational tone. Let the other person(s) speak as well. For every negative, try to give a positive. After the situation is resolved, forgive and forget. No one likes a grudge holder. It's ugly.

- If you have asked a colleague to do something for you and they are unable to get it done, you may need assistance from their superior. If this is the case, have the courtesy to inform your colleague of your plans. You are not running off and "telling on them," you simply need to get something done. Do not be obnoxious about it. No one likes a tattletale.

CUBICLE AND SURROUNDING OFFICE AREA

- Keep your office area clean. If you spill coffee on your desk and floor, do not let it sit and seep into the rug. Clean it up! Dust your area once or twice a week.

- If you have a visitor, do not let them linger around your desk. Your boss will think you are rushing through your work to leave the office early with your guest.

- Take the initiative! If the copier or fax machine is giving you light copies or is constantly jamming, either fix it yourself or call a repair person. Do not walk away or ignore the problem.

- If supplies are low, do not take the last item and wait for some else to restock your supply. Anticipate office needs!

- Keep kitchen area clean.

- Check the stock of supplies in your boss' office. Make sure she has enough of the supplies she uses regularly. Especially note their business card supply, as these may take a week or two to re-order.

MAKE FRIENDS

- When you accept a position, ask permission to take home a company directory to familiarize yourself with those in the office. You should know the company hierarchy by the time you begin your first day.
- Take the initiative to introduce yourself to everyone in your building. This includes the countless daily visitors to your office, i.e., water delivery boy, Federal Express and UPS men, and paper delivery person.
- Respect your colleagues' privacy. You will make friends by not meddling in everyone else's business.

TIP FROM THE TOP: Marsha Fishbaugh, the secretary to Oliver L. North, writes: I strive to make the day smooth and comfortable for those around me. It is impossible to keep all the people happy all the time, but that's my goal. I try to get enough rest at night, and have a polite countenance.

OFFICE GOSSIP AND OTHER USELESS CONVERSATIONS

- Avoid. Period.
- Although you may be drawn into the 10:15 office coffee klatch, remove yourself. An office gossip is a person who wastes a lot of time and is usually untrustworthy.
- You will gain the respect of your boss and colleagues by keeping your mouth shut. This applies to situations both in and out of the office. You never know who is listening.
- Confidentiality is key. Do not discuss company secrets with family and friends.

SUPER SNOOPER

QUESTIONS

- In office meetings, keep your questions organized and to a minimum. No one likes to hear you ramble. If you have many comments, write a memo on your own time.
- If your boss is out of the office and you have to interrupt her via cellular phone or beeper, make sure the question is important and cannot wait until she returns.
- There is a time and a place for every question. If it is Tuesday and you notice your boss has a lunch on Sunday, you do not need to ask her where she would like to go during a busy period of the day. It can wait until later.

TIME

- Always be on time. Period.
- Do whatever it takes to ensure your boss' timeliness.
- Do not abuse your lunchtime. Keep to the time allotted, including the return-from-lunch rest room and kitchen stops.
- Keep a time sheet of the hours you work. Your company may pay you for overtime, and you will need to check these hours against your paycheck.
- Your work hours should be devoted to your office responsibilities. If you need to pay your bills or get other personal work done, do it on your lunch break or after business hours. Do not record these personal hours on your time sheet.

RANDOM TIDBITS FROM THE EXPERIENCED CUBICLE . . .

- Your obligation to proper etiquette and professionalism does not end after your interview.
- Don't drink or do drugs during lunch or anytime it will affect your work.
- You are a representative of your company, department, and boss.
- Do not try to be cute. It is not professional.
- Always make eye contact.
- No screaming, swearing, or throwing things.
- Leave your personal problems at home. The exception to this is a sickness or death in your immediate family. If this is the case, let your boss know what is going on. This may be a good time to use the personal days most companies offer.
- Do not make promises you cannot keep. This includes the timeliness of a document or when your boss can return a call.
- Always be honest, even when you know you can get away with a little white lie. It will come back to haunt you.
- No one likes surprises (unless it involves a box with a big ribbon).
- Learn proper style. I suggest Strunk and White's *The Elements of Style*.
- Be consistent with your work.

CHAPTER TWO

Telephones

The telephone is the lifeline to the outside world. No matter how many calls your office receives in a given day, never let a call drop through the cracks. If you forget that your employer's mother called, it could be the last time you answer the phone in that office! Not to scare you, but the telephone is where it all begins . . .

TELEPHONE ETIQUETTE

Be polite. Be the guard of the office gates. In today's global business world, the telephone has replaced face-to-face meetings. This means the impression you give on the phone could make or break the deal. Think of how many times you have been irritated by a rude voice on the other end of the phone. Most often you decide to avoid calling that person again. This is not a situation that you want to create for people calling in to your office. Even if your boss can't stand the person calling, it does not do you any good to be rude. It is a very small world—this statement is corny

but true! Your boss may be powerful enough to decide who to be nice to and who to shrug off. If you are reading this book, however, then you are an assistant or potential assistant, and it pays to be nice to one and all—you may be working for one of these callers one day! Also, never scream into the phone. You need to be considerate of your co-workers around you. Cubbies are not soundproof! Finally, if you have to make personal calls, keep them brief and do not abuse long-distance privileges.

TIP FROM THE TOP: Sarah Burton works as an executive assistant at BMG, a music licensing company in Los

Angeles. Her boss has a long phone sheet, and the phone never stops ringing. Sarah advises assistants never to sound rushed or crazed on the telephone. She says to give callers the impression that you have everything under control (even if you don't!).

Start by creating a Telephone Etiquette Sheet (Sample 1). Discuss the items with your boss and create an etiquette system that they like.

You will experience many bosses in your career, and they will all have different ways of handling situations and different pet peeves. Some people don't like to keep callers on hold. Other people think they look important if they have twelve callers on hold! Some people always have their assistants say that they are in a meeting when actually they are sitting right there. You must tailor your style to your boss's preferences. Discuss the following with your boss when you first start your job, and then create a sheet that contains the information.

It may seem a bit silly taking the time to write down some of this information. Do it anyway!

This sheet should then be copied and placed in a training file. It will become very useful when you have interns or temporary help in the office—you can hand this sheet to someone new in your office rather than having to explain every procedure.

SAMPLE 1
TELEPHONE ETIQUETTE SHEET

Phone Etiquette Sheet for The Organizer, Rachael Lerner's Office

It is very important to have a pleasant and professional telephone manner in the office. Remember, this is the first impression that people will have of the company . You are in essence the gatekeepers to the company. If you have any questions, it is better to ask someone in the office than keep it to yourself or guess.

TELEPHONE GREETING
"Good morning/good afternoon/good evening, The Organizer."

May I speak with Rachael Lerner?

"May I ask who is calling?" (Get caller's name and the company they are with)

If they give their name but no company, politely ask **"From what company?"**

If they offer no other information, it is then time to ask:

"Will she know what this is regarding?" They will either say yes, or give you a short message about what they need to discuss. After you have *all* of the above information, say:

"Please hold for one moment."

Put the caller on hold and inform your boss of the call. Never leave people on hold for more than a few seconds. If you are getting information for them or someone is about to take the call but not right away, pick up the line and say:

"I am sorry to keep you on hold, Ms. Lerner will be right with you."

WHEN RACHAEL IS ON ANOTHER CALL:
"Rachael is on the other line, may I take a message and have her return the call?"

WHEN RACHAEL IS IN A MEETING:
"Rachael is in a meeting, may I take a message and have her return the call when she is back in the office?"

If the caller asks for a time frame when their call will be returned, give them a realistic answer. The longer you work with your boss, the easier it will be for you to determine this.

AVOIDING A CALLER:
"I am very sorry, Rachael has been very busy this week and is difficult to get on the phone. May I take a message? I will have Rachael return the call when she has a break from her meetings. Unfortunately, it may be later in the week." Even if your boss is avoiding someone, do not make the caller feel like they are being singled out. It is best to make them think that no one has been able to get through to her. Usually, after a few phone calls, the ones that you are trying to avoid will eventually get the point!

(continues)

GETTING YOUR BOSS OFF OF A CALL THAT THEY DON'T WANT TO BE ON:

A good trick is to go to your desk and call your boss in her office from your phone. The caller that she is speaking with will be able to hear the phone ringing. Let it ring for a while, then your boss can sigh in the phone and say:

"I am so sorry, it is crazy here today, my assistant is swamped, I need to pick up this other line. I will have to call you back later."

HOW TO INTRODUCE YOUR BOSS WHEN YOU ARE PLACING OR "ROLLING" CALLS:

"Good morning/good afternoon/ good evening, is Ms. Jean available for Rachael Lerner." Wait until the caller is on the line before patching your boss through (as a general rule, bosses hate to talk to assistants!). If the caller is not available, give your boss the option of leaving a detailed message with the caller's assistant, or if they don't want to, give the other assistant your boss' name, company name, and telephone number.

HOW TO RE-DIRECT A CALL WHEN THE CALLER HAS REACHED THE WRONG DEPARTMENT:

"I am sorry, I can not assist you with that information, you need to speak with someone in the finance department. I will transfer you to Joe Blow in finance and he will be able to help you." Stay on the call until someone in the correct department has answered the phone then say:

"Joe, I have Ms. Smith on the line inquiring about an invoice." Once Joe and the caller are on the line together, then you can hang up. If Joe does not answer, give the caller the direct number to that department and, if available, offer to patch them through to Joe's voice-mail. It may seem like a lot of work for something that does not involve you, but it will make your company look polite and organized!

TO TAKE A COMPLETE MESSAGE YOU MUST GET ALL OF THE FOLLOWING:
- Caller's full name correctly spelled
- Caller's company name
- Caller's telephone number(s)
- Concise message
- Date and time of call

OFFICE INFORMATION
The Organizer
Rachael Lerner's Office
Suite 200
10 Rochester Avenue
Los Angeles, California, 90009
Tel: 310–555–2429
Fax: 310–555–9189
Car: 310–555–6965
Home: 310–555–6925
H Fax: 310–555–7844

IMPORTANT CALLERS THAT ALWAYS GET PUT THROUGH TO RACHAEL
Anna Jean
Renee Rosen
Andrew Steinberg
Jen Levy

YOUR TELEPHONE ETIQUETTE SHEET

- General greeting. _____

_____

- What to say when your boss is on the other line.

_____

- What to say when your boss is in a meeting.

_____

- How to handle a call your boss wants to avoid.

_____

- How to get your boss off of a call that they don't want to be on. _____

_____

- How to "roll" calls (put your boss on the line after you get the correct person on the phone). _____

_____

- How to re-direct a call when the caller has reached the wrong department. _____

_____

- How to take a complete message. _____

_____

- Office address, telephone, and fax numbers. _____

_____

- A short list of callers that should always be put through to your boss *no matter what!* _____

_____

_____

_____

To use this sheet, photocopy at 141%.

TIP FROM THE TOP: Jim Johnson has worked for photographer Matthew Rolston for many years. Matthew is often difficult to reach on the phone because of his hectic shooting schedule. Jim advises assistants to give callers a realistic time frame for when their call will be returned. If your boss is going to be unreachable for a day or two, let the callers know so they don't think that your boss is just blowing them off. No one can be angry with an apology, so apologize for your boss.

THE PHONE SYSTEM

You will save yourself a great deal of time by learning about your office's telephone system. There are several different types of systems, but they usually have similar features. Make it a priority during your first few days in your new office to learn how to use the features listed on the following page. Either use a manual or ask a friendly and patient co-worker to teach you the system. It is best to learn without being asked and without the pressure of your boss standing behind you, waiting impatiently for you to perform a specific task on the phone.

Note the instructions for each feature on the "Telephone Features Cheat Sheet" (sample 2). Make a photocopy and post it next to the phone.

As far as speed dial is concerned, you may want to wait a few weeks before programming in all of the telephone numbers. Take time to familiarize yourself with the people that you have contact with on a daily basis. After you have settled in, you will know which numbers you will be calling frequently and can then program those numbers into your speed dial.

LISTENING IN ON CALLS

In certain industries, nearly the entire day is spent on the telephone—financial firms, advertising agencies, and the entertainment industry, for example. In the executive

SAMPLE 2
TELEPHONE FEATURES CHEAT SHEET

- Transferring _____
- Call Forwarding
- Conference Calling _____
- Voice Mail_____
    - Code _____
    - Skip _____
    - Previous _____
    - Delete _____
    - Save _____
    - Replay _____
    - Edit Greeting _____
    - Transfer to Voice Mail_____
- Intercom _____
- Redial _____
- Mute _____
- Speed Dial
    1. _____
    2. _____
    3. _____
    4. _____
    5. _____
    6. _____
    7. _____
    8. _____
    9. _____
    10. _____

To use this sheet, photocopy at 141%.

offices of many of these companies, the boss handles the majority of his work over the telephone. They meet new clients, discuss projects, make deals, and conduct meetings via conference calls. In these offices the executive assistant listens in on telephone calls. It is important to establish in the beginning if you are allowed to listen in on the calls to your boss. If so, you need to establish guidelines on which calls you should be on. You may not have to listen in on personal calls, no matter how entertaining they might be! If it is decided that you should listen to the phone calls, you will need to get a headset. This allows you to listen to the call, go about your business at your desk, and not be heard by the parties talking on the phone line.

There are advantages and disadvantages to listening in on daily telephone calls. Listening to calls lets you know more of what is going on in your office. You hear firsthand new business, deal making, and meeting planning. It also puts you one step ahead of your boss. If your boss is on the phone with a business associate, promises to send them information, and ends the call by agreeing to meet for lunch soon, you already have two tasks to handle before even being asked. When your boss brings up the phone call, you can present the cover letter to be signed and the lunch date and time already scheduled. By doing tasks before even being asked, you will begin to earn "gold stars."

Okay, listening in on your boss' telephone calls is not all fun and games. Being strapped to your desk on a headset, you do not have the ability to move around the office and handle many of the tasks you have been assigned. It is also difficult to field incoming calls when you are stuck on one taking notes. If you find this to be the case, then it's time to have a little heart-to-heart with your employer. You need to come up with a system whereby your boss can signal to you when he wants you to pick up the line and take notes. There should also be a signal for when you should hang up if you are listening on the call and your boss wants you to get off for whatever reason. This will eliminate the problem of wasting time listening to conversations when you don't need to and give you extra time to get your other work done.

In the end, the advantages of listening in on phone calls usually far outweigh the disadvantages. You can do plenty of things at your desk with the headset on, especially on the computer. You can type memos, organize meetings, work on travel itineraries, and organize meeting agendas. You just need to take advantage of the times your boss is out of the office or in a meeting to complete tasks away from your desk. Remember that it is all about time management!

TRACKING TELEPHONE CALLS

It's nine-thirty and already the phone cord is wrapped around you like a snake! That's great—it means you had a busy morning. To handle all of the telephone calls, you need to keep them organized. You have to create and *constantly update* an organized phone number system, or you will never find anything or anyone. In busy phone offices, computerized phone sheets may be necessary. In other businesses, simple phone logs or message books work well. By incorporating the suggestions below, your phone sheet "gold star" is not far out of your reach! The more organized you are, the bigger the bonus!

TIP FROM THE TOP: Marsha Fishbaugh, secretary to Oliver L. North, keeps a daily log of all incoming calls. Anything that she can handle or pass on to the proper person is not passed on to the boss, but is noted in the phone log. If a situation doesn't warrant his immediate personal attention, it is noted and on his desk at day's end. She also likes to head the page with a "one-liner of inspiration" for the day.

Telephone Sheet

WARNING: This phone-sheet process will only work if your employer acknowledges its existence. You must train them to review it at least once in the morning and once after lunch. If they do not comprehend how invaluable it can be for office communication, you have to sell them on it!

The use of a phone sheet is the most effective way to keep both executive and assistant in sync, and there are a number of computer software programs you can use to create a telephone sheet that works for your office. Stop wincing! It is quite simple for all parties involved. The most important thing to remember about the phone sheet is to always include *all* of the following information:

1. The status of the call (explained below)
2. The caller's name (make sure to ask for correct spelling)
3. The caller's company name
4. Telephone number(s) where the caller can be reached
5. Time and date of call
6. Message, or what the call is regarding

The phone sheet works like this:

1) First thing in the morning, update that day's phone sheet by comparing it to the sheet from the previous day. Any call that was completed can be deleted from the new phone sheet. Any calls that came overnight need to be added right away, including messages on your office answering machine, service, or voice mail. (Most important are the "reminder" messages your employer left for you from home or car in the hours you have been out of the office!) Then print out the phone sheet from the computer. (Sample 3)

2) For the remainder of the day, hand-write on additional phone sheet pages. Blank phone sheet may be photocopied and enlarged to 141% for actual use.

3) Establish a list of abbreviations for your telephone sheet's "Status" section. The following are standard abbreviations used in many offices:

L/W Left Word. This means that your boss called this person and they were not available to take the call. This indicates that they now "owe" your boss a call. (It is similar to a game of tag!)

T/C To Call. This means that your boss has told you that at some point they need to call a specific person. Often your boss will also tell you why they need to call this person. You should write this down in the "message section" preceded by a "re:" for regarding.

RYC Returned Your Call. This means that a caller returned a call from your boss. Most likely, this caller's name will already be on the telephone sheet with a "L/W" in the status section. If your boss takes the call, then that name can be deleted from the phone sheet. If your boss cannot take the call, switch the "L/W" to "RYC." Now the tag game continues and your boss is it!

×2 Times Two. This caller has called twice. Obviously, if the caller has called three or four times, the abbreviation changes to ×3, ×4, etc.

RO Rolodex. This means you should make a note to add the number following this abbreviation to your office Rolodex.

RE: Regarding. This abbreviation is used on everything! It is used on phone sheets and documents to preface a message or a brief summary of what the document is about.

4) Use a highlighter during the day to mark calls that have been completed. A highlighter is more effective than a pen. If you ever need to refer to an old phone sheet, you will be able to read a line that has been highlighted. If it was crossed out by a pen, the information might not be legible.

5) At the end of the day or first thing in the morning . . . the phone sheet cycle starts again. [Go back to step 1, do not pass go, do not collect $200.]

HANDWRITTEN MESSAGE PADS AND LOG BOOKS

In offices where the volume of phone calls is minimal, handwritten memos are sufficient for organizing them. All office-supply stores sell message pads or phone logs. Phone logs are best because they come in books with double or carbon paper. Even after you give your boss a message, a second copy is always in the book. These books can be filed after they are filled and referred to later for misplaced phone numbers or date verifications.

To use a message pad or phone log, simply fill out all the information when someone calls (see Sample 4). It is easy to be lax with these messages and not fill them out completely. *Always fill out the spaces.*

Assign an in-box for the messages and be consistent to avoid confusion and lost messages.

When your boss has returned a call from a message, check off the corner of the message. At the end of the day, these messages can be thrown away, as your message log should already have copies.

SAMPLE 3
COMPUTER PHONE SHEET

DATE	TIME	NAME/CO.	NUMBER	STATUS	MESSAGE/REGARDING
6/1/97	9:15A	BeBe Lerner	310–555–2429	LW	re: Marbles Entertainment deal
6/197	9:21A	Jen Levy	310–555–9778	LW	re: Casting on new film
6/1/97	10:02A	Curtis Knauss	212–555–2866	TC	re: Hyannis Trip
6/1/97	10:18A	David Gregory	213–555–1852	RYC	re: Cannes
6/1/97	10:25A	Pete Albee	916–555–0527	TC	re: PJ Barker
6/1/97	10:45A	Paul Jean	617–555–5975	LW	re: update
6/1/97	11:32A	Mimi McCall	401–555–3643		just saying hello
6/1/97	11:54A	Marius Gallitano	617–555–4121		did you talk to Labamba?
6/1/97	1:30P	Dave Dupuy	310–555–9005	TC	re: new scripts
6/1/97	1:32P	Tim Weaver	617–555–7321	LW	re: new golf course proposal
6/1/97	2:15P	Anthony Fischli	310–555–2561	RYC	re: complaints
6/2/97	9:00A	Jamie Caniffe	213–555–1994	RYC	re: short film location
6/2/97	9:20A	James Marks	213–555–8570	TC	re: interview etiquette
6/2/97	9:45A	Sophie Jean	617–555–5975		when are you going to be back?
6/2/97	10:13A	David Strine	212–555–2745	LW	re: new novel proposal
6/2/97	10:25A	Amanda Dugan	310–555–7398		boxing class starts at 8:30 P
6/2/97	10:35A	Caroline Jenner	212–555–7401	LW	re: Jello recipe
6/2/97	10:52A	Andrew Fisch	617–555–5006		should we meet @ Foxwood
6/2/97	11:20A	John Francis	213–555–6922		I am ready w/male model book
6/2/97	11:28A	George Harbaugh	310–555–1145		How about Tommy's?
6/2/97	12:10A	Jordan Grothe	415–555–8731	TC	re: culinary course
6/2/97	1:35P	Rob Hart	310–555–6479	TC	re: killing spree in Kansas
6/2/97	1:45P	Elise Harte	310–555–4672		pls. call re: Dragon Boat plans
6/2/97	4:35P	Andre Viljoen	213–555–9624	LW	re: Eskimo project
6/2/97	6:15P	Sal Malgunera	617–555–6437		I want to go to Disneyland
6/3/97	9:08A	Jay Ostrawski	213–555–6414		keep writing
6/3/97	10:25A	Doug Rosen	310–555–4545		What do you need?
6/3/97	10:36A	Michael Reardon	617–555–6699	LW	re: Micro Brew deal
6/3/97	11:01A	Phillip Hofmyer	310–555–2747		pls. call re: Doris project
6/3/97	11:15A	Renee Rosen	310–555–4969		pls. call re: bert & ernie
6/3/97	12:20P	Michael Ross	617–555–1739	TC	re: Mayor's meeting
6/3/97	1:00P	Bart Ricards	415–555–9070		pls. call re: San Fran Trip
6/3/97	1:30P	Claire Goodchild	617–555–9848	RYC	re: tripping injury
6/3/97	2:15P	MDA	310–555–4121	TC	re: Hadyn & Chandler
6/3/97	2:18P	Matt Talesfore	213–555–1841	TC	re: Barney's evening gala

PHONE SHEET

DATE	TIME	NAME/CO.	NUMBER	STATUS	MESSAGE/REGARDING

To use this sheet, photocopy at 141%.

FYIs

In addition to tracking phone calls, the phone sheet, message pads, and telephone log books should be used to inform your boss of office activities, meetings, reminders, and miscellaneous information. This eliminates the use of Post-It notes and scrap paper that inevitably get lost in the shuffle (which will always be your fault!).

SAMPLE 4
MESSAGE PAD OR PHONE LOG

MESSAGE

DATE: _____ TIME: _____
FOR: _____
FROM: _____
PHONE#: _____

Telephoned   Please Call
Wants to see you   Will Call Again
Returned your call   URGENT
Was here to see you

MESSAGE: _____
_____
_____

        Taken By: _____

FYIs (For Your Information) are used when you hear something of interest to your boss. You can deal with it, but your boss should be aware. For example, if you are in the office kitchen and overhear someone saying that the CEO's wife is in the hospital after breaking her leg skiing, put a note on the phone sheet, message pad, or log book: "FYI—Mrs. Smith is in the hospital. Do you want to send flowers?" Your boss will then be aware of the situation and be able to inform you how to proceed.

FYIs can also be used for meeting information. If you have scheduled a new meeting or lunch, or a meeting time or location has changed, add that information to the phone sheet starting with "FYI." This way you know your boss has been informed of the meeting status.

Finally, FYIs can be used as reminders. If you notice in the calendar that it is the boss' mother's birthday, put an FYI on the phone sheet and call the florist.

The most important factor in an organized office is good communication between executives and staff. If everyone is informed, the office will run more smoothly and fewer mistakes will be made.

ROLODEXING PHONE CALLS

Part of tracking phone calls is keeping the phone numbers organized. Rolodex systems are essential in all offices. Whichever type you decide to use, make sure it is consistent and easy for other people to understand. There will be times when other people will be working in your office (discussed in Chapter 8). Have an organized Rolodex system so that these people will be able to find the names,

SAMPLE 5
ROLODEX CARD

Lerner, Rachael	O 310–555–4200
VP, Writing Dept.	F 310–555–4201
The Organizer Ltd.	H 310–555–3302
2121 Executive Row	C 310–555–3131
Hollywood, CA 90069	M 310–555–1821

Note the common abbreviations:

| O = Office phone | F = Fax | H = Home phone |
| C = Car phone | M = Mobile | HF= Home fax |

numbers, and addresses needed by your boss. It is also good to note that telephone calls are not the only source of information for your Rolodex. Business cards, letterhead, and e-mail will have information that will need to be put into your office Rolodex. The better you manage and update your Rolodex system, the less time you will have to spend bothering other people for telephone numbers and addresses!

Until recently Rolodex cards were the standard way of organizing phone numbers. This system consists of three-by-five or four-by-six cards that you type or hand-write on and then alphabetize into a rotating holder. (see Sample 5) In some offices just the boss has a Rolodex; in others the assistant has one also. Whichever the case, the main thing to remember is to constantly maintain the

Rolodex. When someone new calls the office, or your boss returns from a meeting with a handful of business cards, immediately put them into the Rolodex(es). If your office has a large number of new contacts and clients on a daily basis, keep a Rolodex folder to file new cards and numbers until you can type them out. (A good project for an intern!)

In today's computer-oriented society, more and more software companies offer computerized Rolodex programs. They improve the old typed-card system tenfold. (see Chapter 5) These systems are fabulous!

Personal electronic organizers have become popular in the last few years. These are like little computer address books and calendars (a.k.a. "brains in a box"). If your boss carries one, remember to update it regularly with the new numbers that have come into the office.

Other people use personal organizers: Daytimer, FiloFax, and Dayrunner are popular brands. Again, it is your responsibility to keep these up-to-date with new names, addresses, phone numbers, and calendars.

IMPORTANT NUMBER CARD

In most offices there are certain numbers that are called all the time (e.g., employer's family members, doctors, lawyers, roadside assistance, Federal Express number, etc.). It may behoove you to create a mini-list of these numbers for your boss. They are sometimes referred to as "important number cards" and are easily created on your computer. After you print these out, they can be laminated and kept in both your boss' wallet and your own.

SAMPLE 6
IMPORTANT NUMBER CARD

Big Boss	O 310–555–1325	Fed Ex # 15–532–5464z
	H 310–555–1555	S.S # 014–66–6666
	F 310–555–1326	AAA # 1–800–888–8888
	C 310–555–9292	Joe Mechanic 213–555–6431
	M 310–555–9453	Boss Jr.'s school 310–555–1122
Mrs. Boss	O 310–555–8854	Babysitter 310–555–6464
	H 310–555–1555	Housekeeper 818–555–1354
	F 310–555–8856	B of A # 0000–000–555
	C 310–555–9293	Passport #0000 0000
	M 310–555–9454	
Ace Asst.	H 310–555–7575	
Dr. Healthy	O 213–555–4643	C 310–555–4625
	H 818–555–4665	M 310–555–0828
Dr. Dentist	O 310–555–4699	H 213–555–6532

CHAPTER THREE

Mail

THE BLUE BOX IS THE MAILBOX. . . .
The first call came into the office at nine-fifteen. The client on the other end of the phone had not received the Federal Express package we sent the night before. There was no need to panic. We would call Federal Express, give them the package tracking number, locate the package, and then call the client back and tell them when to expect its arrival. Before we had a chance to dial, the other phone line rang. It was another client in another city inquiring about their expected package which was also "missing." By eleven, we had three missing Federal Express packages to deal with. We called Federal Express, and they had no record of any of our three packages. "Impossible!" we screamed. We asked our assistant if she remembered putting the packages into the box. "Yeah," she answered, "those three packages you guys gave me yesterday. I put them in the box." We called Federal Express again and asked to speak to a man-

ager. The manager was very polite but not reassuring. "We have no record of these packages. We can't track something that does not exist." The entire day was spent trying to solve this baffling mystery. The clients were upset, we were upset, and Federal Express was fed up with our calls. We decided to redo the packages; our second attempt was successful. Three days passed, and we got a call from the post office. "Are you folks missing some Federal Express envelopes?" the postal employee asked. "We found three packages mixed in with the mail from the mailbox right next to your office. "We confronted our assistant. "Oh, my God," she said. "I must have spaced and put them into the blue box."

TRACKING MAIL

Every day you need to sort through the mail. In some offices, mail comes several times per day. Mail consists of postal mail, inter-office letters, faxes, e-mail, overnight delivery, and messenger packages. You'll need a system to handle the incoming documents:

Step 1. Go through each item, throw away junk mail and flyers, and put papers you are keeping in a separate pile.

Step 2. Papers you keep should be date-stamped. The date stamp indicates the day the item was received in your office, and you can order it from your local office-supply store or, if you have one, the company's supply department. The date stamp should have the name of the person's office as well as a date indicator. There will be situations when it is important to know the exact day that something was received, so do not skip this step.

Step 3. Once you have date-stamped all of the mail, separate mail you can handle from mail for your boss. Prioritize everything for your employer, always keeping in mind that one of your functions is to handle as many tasks as possible (which allows your boss to focus on her job).

This often means you can handle invitations, requests, and informational mailings even if they are addressed to your boss. If it is something you can do, update your boss on a regular basis with the things you are working on and the progress you have made.

TIP FROM THE TOP: Nancy Nemecek worked as an assistant to Michael Eisner. She says that the amount of mail that went through that office was incredible. Absolutely everything was logged into the computer: when it arrived, who sent it, what it was about, where it was filed, and what type of follow-up was required. The assistants in that office also made a photocopy of everything that they gave to their boss. Nancy adds, if the boss takes your only copy of something and then loses it, there is nothing you can do. The best thing to do is make sure there is a backup copy of *everything*.

PERSONAL AND CONFIDENTIAL MAIL

You will sometimes receive mail stamped "Personal" or "Personal and Confidential" (P & C). In most cases leave the envelope unopened in your boss' in-box. You can establish P & C mail procedures with your boss when you first start working. Most people like to open their personal mail themselves. On the other hand, some executives who are very busy rely on their assistant to take care of them in all aspects of their lives, including their personal mail. Either way, don't assume—ask.

THE MAILROOM

You will rely on the people in the mailroom every day during your tenure as an executive assistant. They make sure your packages get out and that your mail gets to you on time! I can not emphasize enough how critical this department is. Be nice! On your first day, make a point of introducing yourself to the mailroom. Likewise, if you have new interns or new assistants, send them down to meet the mailroom. If you work in a large company, it can be helpful for your interns to spend a day in the mailroom shadowing one of the staff. This is a great way to familiarize them with the people in the building and also the schedules that the mailroom follows.

TIP FROM THE TOP: Danny Wantland has run the mailroom at International Creative Management, a large talent agency, for many years. He says that the most common mistake on the part of assistants is that they don't pay attention to the schedules that the mailroom has to abide by. Federal Express, UPS, and messenger services have pick-up times. The mailroom has to have these packages ready at the designated time or the packages won't go out. International packages often have to be in a few hours earlier than domestic packages. Danny suggests that assistants prioritize their days accordingly. If your boss tells you in the morning that you have to get two packages to Japan, four letters overnighted to Boston, and two packages need to go to another office a few blocks away, get the international packages done first. Don't wait until 7:30 P.M. to go yelling into the mailroom that you need to have a package in Japan the next day; they can't do it!

Mail, in and of itself, is not brain surgery. This may be a good task for interns (see Chapter 9) after they have been in your office for a short period of time.

CHAPTER FOUR

Filing

Contracts, letters, faxes, mail, printed e-mails, and inter-office memos create more paperwork than you will know what to do with. One of your primary responsibilities as an executive assistant entails handling the paperwork shuffle. Every piece of paper which comes through your office has a proper place where it should end up—most often in a file. Files will work only if there is a logical system to them. Unless you can quickly find a specific document in your files, there is no point to saving it in the first place.

There are three separate sets of files that should be kept by any office or executive assistant:

- Main files for the office
- Personal files for the boss
- Your personal files

All of these files should be ordered from A-Z. Some people like to make all kinds of sub-categories and extravagant filing systems, but the majority of high-level executive offices stick to the most basic A-Z files. This simply means each file should be labeled clearly and then filed alphabetically. For instance, if you have a client, Joe Smith, the file should be labeled "Smith, Joe" and filed under S. The elaborate filing systems such as color coding are nice but not practical. A-Z files work because they are based on common sense. Anyone coming into your office can easily figure out where to find things.

Within each file are sub-files broken down by project and information. For example, in Joe Smith's file there are

several smaller files. Each file is labeled with the name of each project Joe Smith is working on.

As a basic rule, each individual file should be organized with the most recently dated document on top. Use files with fasteners to keep the documents neat and tidy. Do not overstuff the file—when it is full, make a new file with the same label and add a "File 2."

GENERAL FILES

The first set of files to create are the main files for the office. These include everything related to the actual business that you are running. These files range from clients, projects, general office information, directions to your office, meeting confirmations, company history, office birthday lists, and lists of files that have been archived (banished to storage).

THE BOSS' FILES

The second set of files is for your boss. These should be kept separate from the main files and not as accessible to passersby. Most executives keep these files behind or in their desk, somewhere in their private office. These files include expense reports, salary information, personal medical and dental information, their personal contract with the company, real estate information, and confidential projects.

YOUR FILES

Last, there should be a set of your files, usually located in your desk. Suggestions include vacation ideas, shipping forms, medical and dental forms, fax forms, restaurant lists, personal correspondence, human resources information, and information on using the office technology (e.g., telephone system, fax machine, computer basics, stamp machine, warranties and manuals, etc.)

TRANSITIONAL OR TEMPORARY FILES

Realistically, with the amount of paper that flows through an executive office, you may not be able to get through your to-file pile every day. Even papers that are waiting to be filed need to be organized. This may sound like extra work, but it isn't. Having a desktop file may save your life when your boss is screaming for a copy of the memo that she sent out three days before. A desktop file is a small, expandable file that comes labeled either A-Z or 1–31. Choose whichever works best for you. It is usually easier to have the numbered version because you can file up to a month's worth of documents right at your desk. (If it has been longer than a month since you did your to-file pile, you definitely need an intern!) If you choose to use the A-Z desktop file, then simply file documents alphabetically by project or company name.

Notebooks or three-ring binders can also be used as temporary files. Some executives like to keep the current month's documents within reach. For example, many executive assistants keep current memos from their employer and important e-mails at their desk in a three-ring binder for easy access. Remember, at the end of the month all of these documents need to be transferred to their appropriate place within one of the three main files mentioned earlier.

FOLLOW-UP FILE

This file is a three-ring binder with 31 sections—one for each day of the month. This file should be kept at your desk, since you will use it *all the time*. Use this file to remind yourself of deadlines, meetings, reservations, etc. For example, if you reserve a meeting room with food and audiovisual equipment for a meeting on Friday, you should put a reminder note in the file under the Wednesday before the meeting. When you get to your desk in the morning, one of the first things you should do is look in the follow-up file. A good assistant is organized enough to call and confirm things a few days before they are meant to happen.

RECORD OF FILES

In your computer you should keep a master list of all of the files in the office, broken down into three sections: general files, boss files, and your files. Every time you create a new file, take two seconds and add it to the list in the computer. This will help you stay extra-organized, and it will also make the project of storing and purging files much easier.

STORAGE

Every six months you need to go through the files (I'm sensing an intern project . . .) to see what can go into storage. Print out the master list of general files and your boss' files from your computer. Drop the lists into your boss' in-box. They can then highlight the files that can be put into storage. Usually these are files of projects that have been finished or canceled. You can decide on your own files yourself. Every local business-supply store sells boxes specifically designed for file storage. Make sure to label all sides of the box clearly and put a contents page inside the lid of each box. A copy of these contents pages will go into your main files under "storage." This will help you keep track of every document that entered your office.

TIP FROM THE TOP: In the office of Larry Murphy (Senior Vice President and Chief Strategic Planning Officer) at the Walt Disney Corporation, the two executive assistants use their boss' vacation week to purge the office files. They bring in one of their regular temporary assistants who is familiar with their office (from working during the rare times when one of the permanent assistants is out sick or on vacation). This temp provides extra help for the task of cleaning up and organizing the files. The three women spend the entire week going through each filing cabinet and organizing. It would be far too hectic to attempt this project with their boss in the office, so his vacation week is the ideal time.

FILERS

Filing is a task that is often handed down to interns and office assistants. If you have someone else filing for you, follow a few basic rules:

- Take the time to go through your system with them, showing them *all* of the filing cabinets. Make sure they understand how your files are organized.

- Supervise. This means that you should check on their progress and make sure that paperwork is ending up where it should.
- Have realistic expectations of how much filing can be done in one day. If you overwhelm people with filing, they are more likely to get frustrated and start shoving papers into files just to make their piles smaller. This inevitably leads to lost paperwork.

TIP FROM THE TOP: Renee Rosen, executive assistant to Stacey Snider at Universal Pictures, gives her filers extra help. She separates the papers that need filing into the following categories: legal/business affairs, notes, lists, coverage, and correspondence. Her filers are then able to file the documents in the correct files without having to decipher which type of document it is. This may seem like a little extra work, but it is worth it. Often you will have new interns or assistants filing for you. If they are not used to reading business documents, they might not know which type it is. Unfortunately, some people will stick a document anywhere when they don't know where it goes rather than asking. With this system you don't leave room for guesswork and will be able to find the documents when you need them.

CHAPTER FIVE

Computers

Be not afraid! Embrace computers. Welcome them into your life with open arms, like an old friend. If you take the time to learn how to manipulate them, your office will run at a much higher efficiency level.

It is impossible to explain here every type of computer and software program. There are hundreds of books outlining the vast software options in great detail. The purpose of this chapter is to help you organize and work with the system already in place in your office and give you the basic tools necessary to have a computer-oriented office.

STEP ONE: INTRODUCE YOURSELF TO THE COMPUTER GEEKS

Does your company have a computer department full of well-trained individuals, ready to help you with your office computer woes? If so, send them a gift basket of beer from whatever hip micro brewery has popped up in your part of the world. These people will soon become your new best friends. They can help create templates, back up your computer, set up e-mail, install new programs, and most important, come to your aid when you think you may have accidentally erased that fifty-page report! If you get nothing else out of this chapter, please heed this advice: befriend the computer department!

TIP FROM THE TOP: Dan Miller works at a major New York publishing house in the computer department, and he offers the following advice on getting on the good side of the help desk:

Learn how to log on properly to your computer and your boss' computer. This means remembering your password, your boss' password, and how to change passwords. According to Dan, the most common problem that he is asked to fix involves assistants who don't log onto their computers correctly.

Don't try to impress them with what you know about computers. They know more! If you approach them with a humble attitude, "I don't know how to do this, can you teach me?", they will gladly take the time to show you the ropes.

Don't try to impress them with how important your boss is. They don't care! If you are nice to them, they will be more likely to assist you in your emergency rather than another assistant who leaves screaming messages saying "Mr. Jones needs his computer fixed *now!*"

Create a reputation as an assistant who learns after the first mistake. That way, they won't mind showing you *once*, knowing you will not call a hundred times with the same question.

When they do come up to your office in response to a repair call, do not leave them waiting while you finish phone calls and various other tasks. They are busy too!

STEP TWO: KNOW YOUR COMPUTER

If you don't understand computers very well, have the computer department teach you. It is important to understand the properties of your office computer system. If your company has a computer department, you will not have to handle some of the tasks following. If you work in a smaller company, you will need to take the responsibility of maintaining your computer. Make a point of knowing the answers to the following questions:

Your Computer Information

- What is the model and brand of your computer?
- How much memory does your computer have?
- What versions of software does it run?
- With what systems is it compatible?
- Are you linked up to a network or are you on an independent computer?

- What printer(s) is your computer hooked up to?
- If you are on a network, does the computer department automatically back up the system?
- Are you responsible for backing up your own system?
- Does your network offer in-house e-mail, outside e-mail, Internet access?
- If you are on a network, is there a special place that you should store your documents?
- Is the computer under warranty?
- How much longer does this warranty last, and what does it cover?

Basic Software

There are two programs that are essential to your office computer: word processing and a spreadsheet program. Hundreds of companies offer these programs with a slew of promises about their special capabilities. When choosing word processing and spreadsheet software, ask yourself the following questions:

- Does it have the features that are sync with your needs (spell check, mail merge, templates, labels, etc.)?
- Is it compatible with the software other people in the company use?
- Is it compatible with the software the people you do business with use?
- Does the software company upgrade their software, continually improving it and adding new features?
- Does the software come with technical support (i.e., understandable manuals and customer support telephone numbers?)

- Is it compatible with other software programs that you have on your system?

As an executive assistant, you will rely heavily on these two software programs. Make your life a little easier and choose the best ones. According to all of the assistants interviewed for this book, Microsoft Word and Microsoft Excel are the most popular programs on the market, with Word Perfect and Lotus 1,2,3 also getting good mentions.

Once you have a word processing and spreadsheet program, take the time to familiarize yourself with *all* of the features available on your software. Then take the time to master the features that are useful in your type of office. For example:

WORD PROCESSING PROGRAM
- Templates for business letters, fax cover sheets, memos, and form letters
- Labels
- Envelopes
- Tables

SPREADSHEET PROGRAM
- Expense reports
- Mileage reports
- Budgets
- Profit and loss reports
- Charts and graphs

Many of the software programs on the market have a file with sample documents in them which can assist you in creating your own templates for all of the above functions.

INTERMEDIATE SOFTWARE

After you are comfortable with your basic programs, you will be ready to graduate to the next step. The following programs are not necessary for office survival, but are very useful.

SCHEDULING PROGRAM

You will be at the top of your game if you have a calendar or scheduling program. You'll know exactly where your boss is at any given moment, or at least where she was supposed to be. The programs we give a warm welcome to are Now Up-to-date, and Microsoft Outlook.

Both of these programs have a detailed day, week, and month scheduler to allow you to plug in your boss's meetings. Also, you could keep a calendar of client appointments, office birthdays, personal friend birthdays, anniversaries, etc. If you are on a network, you can update schedules on your computer, and your associates and boss will be able to look at the updates on their computers.

ROLODEX PROGRAM

As was briefly discussed in the Telephone chapter, it is time to get your Rolodex off your desk and into your computer. Rolodex program suggestions include In Touch, Quickdex, and Filemaker Pro. The only hassle is inputting the information from a vast stack of cards. However, you will find as you sift through the cards that most are either outdated or duplicates. You'll be able to weed out useless cards and become more familiar with the contents of your Rolodex. Once all of the information has been properly loaded, the computer will get the information faster than it would have taken to look up the number the old-fashioned way. If you forget part of the information (e.g., the full name or company), you can use the bits of information you do remember to have the computer search for you. For example, the boss shouts, "Get me that man who installed my doggy door!" You only remember the company was in Schenectady. Type in Schenectady into the computer and *voilà*, it gives the listings of all the people in the Rolodex from Schenectady. You then flip through the ten or so listings until you find the number for Mr. Doggy Door installer. It's that simple! Had you been using the old system, you'd still be searching now and not have the time to read this book!

These computer programs also have the capability of creating lists, such as birthday and Christmas card lists. A few popular programs can print labels directly from the Rolodex for mailings. Whichever type of office you are in, a computerized Rolodex system will always improve its efficiency.

ADVANCED SOFTWARE

Okay, you are a genius (either that, or you have far too much time on your hands)! You are now ready to move all the way up to the advanced programs. Advanced does not necessarily mean they are more difficult to use. Compare it to eating dessert. Dessert is not harder to eat than the main course; it just depends on how much room is left in your stomach! If you have extra time and ambition, the following programs are worth adding to your computer system.

ACCOUNTING PROGRAM

Please do not run away! This is not a book for CPAs. Accounting programs are useful for us everyday folks as well. You need to learn only the basics of these programs. Do not worry if the rest of the instruction manual looks like it is in a foreign language. You can use an accounting program to track your department's petty cash, travel expenses, and your personal office expenses. These programs can help balance your checkbook, cut checks, and report how much you are spending on what. If you decide to purchase accounting software, call the company accounting department and ask them what software they use. This will ensure that you get software that is compatible with theirs. Again, this program is not absolutely essential to having an organized office; you can definitely get by without it. But if you have the extra time, it can help make you that much more organized.

PAINT/DRAW PROGRAM

It is acceptable to work and have fun while you are doing it. In fact, let me take a moment to encourage you to enjoy your job! If you have the opportunity, pick up a paint/draw program and have a little fun with your work. Corel Draw, Adobe Illustrator, and Microsoft Powerpoint are a few of the great programs available

that allow you to have some creative fun while you're doing work at the same time. They allow you to create presentations and documents with free-hand drawing and color. Most are very user friendly, and you can actually teach yourself by playing around with them in your spare time. These programs give you the ability to start with a blank page, like an easel, and create from there. You can import documents from other programs such as a word processing document or spreadsheet, and add color and design to make your presentation that much more impressive.

E-MAIL

Hello, it is almost the year 2000! If you are not hooked up to e-mail yet, get with it! My mother is in her late sixties and she just got e-mail (okay, give me a break, I had to mention my mom at least once in this book). E-mail allows you to write to someone on your computer, press a Send button, and *voilà*! They get your message right away. This is the ultimate way to cut down on your phone bill. Some offices that are on a network (all the computers are linked together) have an in-house e-mail system. This means that you can "talk" amongst your office staff from your computer to theirs.

For e-mail that the rest of the world has access to, you will need:

- A computer
- A telephone line
- Modem
- E-mail software
- An Internet service provider

Okay, if you have a computer expert handy, have them set up your e-mail and skip the rest of this section. If you are going to tackle this one on your own, don't sweat it, it isn't that hard. Ask around the office for a good Internet service provider in your area. Call them up and tell them that you want to set up an Internet account. They will ask you for your name, address, phone number, and phone number to the extra line that you are going to use for the computer. They will charge you a monthly fee. They will also send you the software that you need to install in your computer. Finally, they will give you a log-in name, a password, and instructions for setting up your computer to dial into their information bank. That's it. Easy as one, two, three! Now you can talk to all of your friends and business associates around the world without paying a hefty phone bill. If you get "hooked up," you have just won the lottery, because not only do you have e-mail access you also have access to. . .

THE INTERNET

That's right, folks, welcome to cyberspace! The Internet is a library (the biggest) of information. People are able to get a site, or address, on the Internet. If you type that address into your computer, you can read whatever information that site provides. There are several Internet browsers that let you search for specific topics and provide you with the addresses of the sites that interest you. Access to the Internet is one thing that I highly recommend you get. However, you may want to search the net at home because it can be addicting and time-consuming. It is very hard to go back to your boring report when you are reading about scuba diving expeditions in Boracay! Because you want to keep your job, refrain from surfing the net when you are supposed to be typing a memo.

BACKING UP YOUR COMPUTER

This is very important: Computers are not fail-safe. They can do magic, but they can also crash!

Find out if your computer department backs up your computer on a regular basis or if you are responsible for this task.

Backing up simply means copying all the information on your computer's hard drive onto disks to keep in the event of a computer crash, power failure, or other natural disaster. If you have all of the original disks for your software programs, then there is no need to copy all of the programs, just copy your files. *Do this regularly*. In other words, set up a schedule and stick to it. The pain that you suffer by taking the time to copy your files onto disks is significantly less than the pain you will suffer if all of your information is lost. Trust me. If you do not know how to back up your system, ask the computer department, your friend, or anyone who knows how to do it. Repeat, this is very important.

REBOOTING YOUR COMPUTER

Rebooting (shutting down and then restarting) your computer is a good way to keep your computer running smoothly. It is sort of like a "nap" for your computer, allowing it to purge, clean itself up, and then start all over again. A common mistake that people make is to have their computer running with fifteen programs open on the desktop. This slows the whole system down and increases the chances of a computer crash.

UPDATING YOUR COMPUTER

When you become a really advanced computer user, you may be ready for updating. Computer technology is constantly changing and improving. Chances are, there are improvements that can be made to your computer without replacing it. You can expand the memory, increase the speed, and add extra features. If you have paid attention and established a good relationship with the computer boys downstairs, ask them about updating your system. If a computer department does not exist in your company, visit your local computer superstore. Be sure to know your computer manufacturer and model before you go asking questions.

TIP FROM THE TOP: A friend of mine works for Warner Bros. She continually improves her computer skills by taking courses provided by her company. The courses are short (one to two days) and free to anyone who works at her company. Check with your human resources department to see if your company offers computer courses. If not, ask if they have a tuition-reimbursement program whereby you can take a course at a local university and be paid back by your company.

ORGANIZING YOUR COMPUTER DESKTOP

Your computer should be organized. The desktop layout should be orderly and have clearly labeled computer files for:

- Office
- Clients
- Boss
- You

Having the computer organized is as important as having paper files and Rolodexes organized. If you are absent for a day, be it a vacation or sickness, the office will be set up so other people, (i.e., a temp or intern) could easily find everything necessary to run the office smoothly.

Office Files

- Fax cover sheet template
- Letter from your boss' template
- Memo template
- Letter from your template
- Training files
- Mailing labels
- Mailing lists
- Phone lists
- Cheat book information (see chapter 13)

Client Files

Every client or business associate should have his or her own file in the computer. These files should contain everything needed to do business with them, broken down into sub-files as follows:

- Correspondence
- Meetings
- Agendas
- Meeting minutes/notes
- Submissions
- Miscellaneous (this means one file titled "Miscellaneous," not lots of miscellaneous files!)

The Boss' File

Keep a separate file on your boss, containing all of her personal documents and information. Break these files down into sub-files suited to her needs.

Examples for boss' files:

- Travel itineraries
- Expense reports
- Personal correspondence
- Doctor lists
- Emergency numbers
- Mailing lists
- Résumés
- Miscellaneous

Your File

Finally, there should be a separate file for you. Who knows? You may get a moment to do something for yourself in your fourteen-hour day. I suggest the following file subcategories:

PERSONAL CORRESPONDENCE
- Résumé/bio
- Inter-office memos
- Miscellaneous

RESOURCES

But you still have one question. . . . I know, I always do, too. There are a few different ways of handling questions about your computers and software. If you are one of those lucky individuals who has a new best friend in the computer department, take advantage of them. It's what they are paid to do. They can help with technical problems such as replacing broken computer parts, and they can create original templates for forms and documents that are specific to your work (very nice to have). This service is very important!

Another resource for computer questions and problems is the 800 numbers provided by computer and software companies. These numbers connect you to a support team of people trained specifically to guide you through computer and software problems. You could be on hold for several minutes before a live person comes on the line. Be sure to ask as many questions as you need to, and don't feel like you are forced to say, "Yes, I understand," if you don't. They are paid to answer *all* of your questions, no matter how small.

When you purchase new software, fill out the registration card which accompanies it. The 800 number helpers will ask for a registration number before answering your question(s).

A third resource is the manual that accompanies your computer or software. These are as useful to most people as instructions to programming a VCR or assembling anything from Ikea. If you feel the urge to try the manuals, best of luck to you. They are often difficult to comprehend. These manuals were written by the same people who do the actual programming of the software. In other words, they aren't written in laymen's terms.

The fourth resource you will have to find on your own. It is a person who can sit and hold your hand (the other one) while you type away. This poor soul could be a friend who knows "all about computers" or a computer super-store employee who can help you with your computer-oriented issues.

TIP FROM THE TOP: According to Craig Gunther, who works in the computer department at International Creative Management (a top talent agency) one of the most common frustrations that his department has with assistants is they do not listen when they are asking for help. When you are seeking assistance from a computer expert, you shouldn't be doing all of the talking. Explain what the problem is (the screen is frozen, a document won't open, etc.) and then let them explain what steps you can take to mend the situation. If someone is taking the time to help you with your computer woes, watch what they are doing, hopefully you can fix the problem yourself should it happen again.

It may seem scary at first, but the computer will be the most loyal and useful partner in your job. Face your fears and start tackling cyberspace.

CHAPTER SIX

Meetings and Scheduling

ALWAYS ASK—Here's the story of one executive assistant who learned the hard way:

The agent that I was working for asked me to set up a meeting with several in-house agents (whom he listed for me) and the head of one of the major television networks. This was going to be a very important meeting for the agency, an opportunity to introduce new talent and ideas for TV movies and TV series. Without really thinking too much about it, I called the network executive's assistant to set up the meeting. We came up with a few dates that accommodated her boss and my boss. I told her I needed to confirm with the other attending agents, and I would call her back. I sent out an e-mail to the assistants of the other in-house agents, and we agreed upon a date. I called the network executive's assistant and told her which date and time we had chosen. "Great" I said, "We're all set for Tuesday, 4:00 P.M., here at the agency." The other assistant hesitated for a moment and then in a slightly meek voice replied, "Okay, he'll be there, thanks." Looking back, I wish I had recognized the change of tone in her voice. Not more than a few minutes after we hung up the phone, it rang again. It was a call from the agency boardroom upstairs. I answered the phone and could barely make out anything through the ear-piercing screams. The head of my boss' department was calling from the boardroom in the middle of her "very important meeting." Apparently, her office received a call from the network executive himself. When he was told that the agent was in a meeting, the network executive asked that it be interrupted. Upon being connected, the network executive told the agent that an assistant in her department had the nerve to schedule a meeting between such and such people at the agency, not at his office at the network. "How could you be so stupid?" the agent screamed at me. "Since when do network executives conduct meetings at someone else's office? They don't travel to us, we travel to them!" Like I knew! It seemed logical to me that a meeting consisting of six people in one building and one person in another building would take place in the building where the majority of attendees worked. The meeting was rescheduled to take place at the network. There were no other flaws. I quickly learned, Never assume. If you do not know, then ask."

SETTING UP MEETINGS

A quick checklist for setting up meetings:

1. Participants (who, status)
2. Location, date, and time
3. Confirmations
4. Meeting Agenda

PARTICIPANTS

The first thing to know when setting up a meeting is who the participants are. Though it seems ridiculous to say that the first step in arranging a meeting is to ask your boss who should be at the meeting, it is truly the most important step, just so you do not leave someone out. A side note: if all of these people are not in the Rolodex, they should be. You will probably be doing future business with them.

If you're not familiar with the participants and their status, then you need to find out. Ask your boss who the most important participant is and then work everything else out around that person's schedule, according to what would be most convenient for him or her. Some people are more important than others as far as business rank. They need to be the first considered for time and location of the meeting. This does not necessarily mean that this person is the most important attendee in the grand scheme of things, but rather is the most critical person in terms of your boss' goals for the meeting.

EXAMPLE:

You could be setting up a meeting involving Bob Dole and Leona Helmsley. You might assume that Bob is more important because he once ran for the presidency and was a lifelong senator who served our nation, but never assume. In actuality, the purpose of your boss's meeting is to get Leona to donate one of the ballrooms in the Waldorf Hotel for a charity event. Bob is to be the guest speaker. According to your boss, it is more important to solidify the ballroom than the speaker. Therefore, Leona is more important for this meeting. In this case, Leona should be the person first asked about her schedule.

LOCATION, DATE, AND TIME

Once you know who will be attending the meeting and their status, you can choose a location that is convenient for the most important attendee. After the participants and the location have been decided, you need to choose a time. Busy executives hate to waste time sitting in traffic for hours during a workday to get to a meeting. Look at the location and date of the meeting, and come up with a time that is considerate of all the people in the meeting, especially your boss. For example, if your office is in midtown Manhattan, scheduling a meeting for your boss in Long Island on a Friday at 3:00 P.M. is not a good idea. Your boss will be stuck in weekend traffic on the way there and back. Traffic will probably take extra hours out of her day. If that meeting was on a Tuesday morning at 11:00 A.M., the chances that travel to and from the meeting will be fairly smooth are much better than your Friday meeting. Anticipating the duration of a meeting is also important. You should always ask the person who wants to schedule a meeting how long they think the meeting will last. Likewise, when your boss calls a meeting, you should include the anticipated duration on the confirmations before you send them out.

CONFIRMATIONS

The final and often most important step in organizing a meeting is to fax confirmations to every single participant. Confirmations should be filed in a folder with the name and date of the meeting printed on the label. This confirmation should contain all of the following meeting information:

- Title/purpose of meeting
- Date
- Time
- Location
- Participant names
- Directions to the meeting from major freeways, including exact address of meeting (suite or room number) and phone number to meeting room
- Contact phone numbers
- Indicate on confirmation if food is involved: breakfast, lunch, or snacks
- Duration of the meeting

Make sure to send one confirmation to the actual meeting location site to make sure that the people at that location know how many people are involved, etc. Also, if there is any special equipment needed at the meeting room (audiovisual, etc.), this should be noted on the confirmation. Confirmations are essential to making sure that any meeting runs smoothly. By confirming, everyone involved has been given the specifics, and it takes the responsibility off you. That is why it is critical to save these faxes once you have sent them out with the fax transmittal confirmation attached to it. If Joe Schmoe does not show up at the meeting or goes to the wrong location, you have proof that you gave him the proper information. Believe me, when something goes wrong, you are the first person accused of messing up. Having all of your documentation filed is a way of covering your back and defending yourself.

MEETING AGENDA

The last part of scheduling a meeting is the creation of a meeting agenda. You are only responsible for the agenda if your boss is the one calling the meeting. If she is the head of the meeting, then she will be able to give you the topic or reason for the meeting and a list of the things that need to be discussed. This list should be typed out in the following order:

- Meeting title
- Attendees
- Outline of topics that need to be covered

Agendas should be given out at the beginning of the meeting. They will help the meeting run in a smooth and orderly fashion. Please note, if more than one person from your company is going to attend the meeting, your boss may want them to contribute to the meeting agenda. If so, you should let them know a few days before the meeting to allow them time to pull their information together.

TIP FROM THE TOP: Sarah Burton works for a busy executive at BMG in Los Angeles. She advises assistants to keep in mind that schedules change. Don't expect anything to stick, and use pencil when writing in your boss's calendar because you will erase each entry at least twice! Don't get flustered if you've worked on setting up a meeting and it gets changed; you work for an executive, it will happen often!

MAINTAINING AN ORGANIZED SCHEDULE

As most people know, time management is one of the keys to success. Your job as an executive assistant is just as it sounds, to assist an executive. You need to be the keeper of the clock and help organize her day in a fashion that allows for the greatest productivity and use of every minute possible.

When you begin your new job, you must master your boss' scheduling system. Different systems include computer scheduling software, personal day planners, and desk calendars. If you can get your boss to adopt the computer system, do it. It is the most efficient way of scheduling. (see Chapter 5) Unfortunately, there are still people out there who are afraid of technology. If one of those people happens to be your boss, sorry, but you will just have to deal with it!

Take a little while to figure out your boss and the pace at which she likes to work—how many meetings a day does your boss like to have? How many breakfast, lunch, or dinner meetings per week should you schedule? This will give you something to work with when planning the day-to-day life of your employer.

When you schedule meetings, breakfasts, lunches, or dinners, make sure that these events are written down in the appropriate places. They should be in a calendar at your desk and also in your boss' calendar. It is always wise to let your boss know when you have scheduled a meeting. A phone sheet is a good way of communicating this information to your boss. (see Chapter 2)

In some offices, executive schedules need to be circulated to other executives so that all of the top brass within the company are aware of their colleagues' agendas. If this is the case, you should do this at a scheduled time each week. Make sure your calendar is orderly and legible before sending it out to other offices.

RESTAURANT/LOCATION LIST

Create a list of places your boss likes to use for meetings and meals, for both personal and business matters, as well as her dietary restrictions, including food allergies.

This list should be put in your personal files under

"restaurant lists," in your main files under the same title and in your cheat book (see Chapter 13). This list should be detailed enough to enable any temp working in your office to figure it out and schedule a restaurant meeting for your boss without asking them any questions. Each listing should show the restaurant name, the maître d' or manager's name and direct-dial phone number, the location, the travel time to and from the office, and your boss' favorite items served. Establish relationships with people at these locations, i.e., the maître d' at her favorite lunch spot. These will be extremely valuable connections, and will often help in a crunch.

TIP FROM THE TOP: Renee Rosen, executive assistant to Stacey Snider at Universal Pictures, goes by the five-meeting-per-day rule. A lunch meeting is included as one of the five meetings. This simply means that she never schedules more than five meetings per day for her boss. If you schedule too many meetings, your boss will never have time at her desk to get work done. This will translate into late hours for you and a grumpy employer. If you do have a busy five-meeting day scheduled, make certain that all the meetings are not at other people's offices. You must take into account travel time to and from each meeting.

PERSONAL SCHEDULING

Scheduling your boss' personal life may or may not be your responsibility. Some top executives have an assistant that deals strictly with personal matters. Other executives, believe it or not, actually schedule their own personal itinerary. For most, however, you will be the one who handles their personal schedule. Treat this scheduling and planning just as you would for business and confirm everything via phone and fax.

ESCAPE SCENARIOS

Finally, create escape scenarios with your employer. These are to be used only in emergency situations or when your boss tells you that they do not want to be in a particular meeting for more than a specific amount of time. Discuss these escape scenarios with your boss and come up with several different situations. For example, your boss is having lunch with a client in which she has no interest, but she was told by *her* boss that she had to attend. Your boss is very busy during this particular week and has instructed you to get her out of the lunch after twenty minutes. You wait *exactly* twenty minutes and then you call the restaurant. You inform the maître d' to bring a note to your boss' table. The note says that an important conference call has been moved to an earlier time due to the other company's president's schedule and your boss needs to return to the office right away. This is called an escape scenario, and because you have already discussed this with your boss, she will know that it is not a real emergency. This leaves her free to decide if she still wants to leave her lunch early.

MEETING CHEAT SHEET

YOUR BOSS:

Number of meetings per week _____

Number of breakfasts per week _____

Number of lunches per week _____

Number of dinners per week _____

Favorite restaurants, contact person, and favorite food items:

1. _____

2. _____

3. _____

4. _____

5. _____

Food Allergies _____

_____

Escape Scenarios:

1. _____

2. _____

3. _____

4. _____

5. _____

To use this sheet, photocopy at 141%.

CHAPTER SEVEN

Travel and Itineraries

SCREAMING FROM THE PLANE—Although employers often hate to admit it, they would not know how to button their shirts without us. Here's one assistant's story:

The phone rang at 6:30 A.M. as I was house-sitting for my boss. He was on a multi-country vacation, about three-quarters through his trip, and was calling from an airplane, screaming about a missing ticket. After boarding his flight, he realized that he had left the remainder of his airline ticket at a friend's house. During his layover, he went to the nearest ticket counter and proceeded to pay full price for a same-day flight in first class! It cost him almost $3,000. Had he called me first, I would have explained to him that there is a logical procedure on most airlines for lost tickets. He could have gone to the ticket counter, told them he had lost his ticket, shown some identification, paid a small lost-ticket fee, and been issued a new ticket. Unfortunately, like many of the people that I have worked for, he preferred to take the hardest route out of a situation and then spent his remaining energy yelling at me. I eventually resolved this problem by calling a friend in special services at the airline who allowed me to file a lost-ticket report after the fact. We had to wait six months, but the ticket was eventually reimbursed.

TRAVEL

Coordinating travel is probably the toughest part of an executive assistant's job. One would think that it is great to get your boss out of the office for a while when, actually, it is usually a nightmare! Travel involves even more organization than usual. You need to think of *everything* before it happens. My advice is to enact the entire trip from morning to night in your head as if you were there with your boss. Ask yourself, What will she need for this lunch or this meeting? How far away is the next meeting? How will she get from point A to point B? Think of everything! The first trip that you plan for your boss will be the toughest.

The Travel File

As soon as you hear that your boss has to travel, make two folders labeled with the location and date of the trip—one for you and one for your boss. When you schedule a meeting, immediately ask your boss if there is any paperwork for that meeting. After she gives you the papers, put them right into her folder. Make a copy of any confirmation letters for airline, transportation, and hotels, and put one in her folder and one in your folder. As soon as you receive the airline tickets, put them into her folder. Keeping all travel documents organized and in one place helps not only with making the traveling plans, but it will also keep you from forgetting to give something to your boss when she leaves. Keep all of your notes from the first trip handy, and refer to them for all subsequent travel. These notes will help you when you are making arrangements for airlines, transportation, and hotels. Always keep a file for every trip to refer back to at a later date.

Itineraries

The secret to an organized and successful business trip is the "working" itinerary. (see Sample 7) The minute you learn of a trip, create a computer file for that trip. Anytime

SAMPLE 7
TRAVEL ITINERARY

Jane Smith's Itinerary–X City 9/30/96

Monday, 9/30/96

8:00 A.M.	Leave house in own car for Airport
	At Airport take first right off Airport Road to Lot C parking
10:00 A.M.	Leave LAX Airline #1111
3:00 P.M.	Arrive X City
	Limos Are Us will meet you at gate and drive you to Hotel
	Limos Are Us–Confirmation #111111
	Limos Are Us–Telephone /Contact 617–555–5555 / Julie Limo
	Travel time: 15 min./6 miles
	Hotels Are Us
	100 Hotel Road
	Hotel City, XX, 00000
	508–555–5555 Phone
	508–555–5515 FAX
	Confirmation number #222222
5:00 P.M.	Limos Are Us pick up @ Hotel
	Confimation #111112
	Travel time: 5 min/1.5 miles
5:30 P.M.	Drinks with Joe Smith & Bob Jones of Smith & Jones Corp.
	Drinks Are Us
	10 Drunk Lane
	Drink City, XX 00001
	Drinks Are US 310–555–5555 Phone
	310–555–5515 Fax

	Joe Smith's office 310–555–0239 Phone
	310–555–0238 Fax
	Bob Jones' Office 310–555–0231 Phone
	310–555–0232 Fax
	Reservation under: Jane Smith
	Contact: Pierre/Bar Manager

7:15 P.M.   Leave Drinks Are Us and walk one building East to

7:30 P.M.   Dinner with Sue Smith & Jane Jones of Sue & Jane Corp.
Fancy Dinners Are Us
12 Drunk Lane
Drink City, XX 00001
Fancy Dinner's 310–555–5556 Phone/310–555–5557 Fax
Sue & Jane Corp.   310–555–7777 Phone/310–555–7779 Fax
Reservation under: Sue Smith
Contact: Claude/Maitre'd

10:00 P.M.   Limos Are Us pick up @ Fancy Dinners Are Us and return to Hotel
Confirmation #111113
Travel time: 5 min./1.3 miles

Tuesday, 10/1/96

6:00 A.M.   Limos Are Us pick up @ Hotel to X City Airport
Confirmation #111114
Travel time: 15 min/6 miles

7:15 A.M.   LV X City Airline # 2222

2:45 P.M.   AR LAX
Exit terminal and take shuttle bus to Lot C to retrieve your car
(Overnight charge $8.00)

(continues)

Meetings to Set:

Pete Peters of Peter Company	555–555–5555
Sally Sue of Sally Sue Productions	555–557–5555

Contact Numbers:

Assistant (your) numbers	555–444–5555 home
	555–444–5553 cellular
	555–444–5552 direct office
	555–444–5151 fax
Mary Jones in X City Office	555–444–5522 direct office
	555–444–5556 fax

that you make a reservation or schedule a meeting, add it to the itinerary along with all pertinent information about that meeting, including location, travel distance, date, time, people attending, telephone and fax numbers. At the bottom of your itinerary, keep a list of "meetings to set," that is, people that your boss wants to see during her trip. List their names, companies, and phone numbers. As soon as a meeting time has been confirmed, delete it from the "meetings to be set" section and add it to the appropriate time slot with all of the necessary meeting information. When you make or are informed of a meal reservation, make a note in the itinerary with the restaurant contact name and the name the reservation is under. Another item to add to the bottom of the itinerary is a "contact number" section, starting with your numbers, followed by anyone else that is assisting with this trip, (e.g., an executive secretary or meeting planner in the destination city.)

Airlines

Many people prefer to fly on one airline because they can accumulate frequent-flier miles and earn free trips. Not all airlines, however, fly to every city.

You should make a list of three airlines that your boss likes and use her number one choice whenever possible.

It is also important to find the most direct flights to each destination. No one enjoys layovers and changing planes.

If you are working within a large company, there is probably an in-house travel service to help you make reservations for your boss. If there isn't, shop around until you find a travel agency that suits your needs. *This will be one of the key relationships to establish in your new job.* It is *extremely* important to have a great working relationship with whichever travel service you use. (Flowers, restaurant gift certificates, and certificates to a day spa are just a few suggestions for gifts you should lavish upon them.) I have worked for many busy executives who change their plans every five minutes and schedule trips at the last second. If you have a strong relationship with a travel agent or your in-house travel service, these last-minute changes will be a little less stressful.

TIP FROM THE TOP: Deena Whitesman is a travel agent at New Act Travel in Los Angeles. She handles many big executives and celebrities. Her advice: Know the dates—and especially the times—of your boss' travel when you call. There are often several flights per day to certain cities; you should know if your boss wants to leave in the morning, afternoon, or evening. Also, when your boss cancels a trip, make sure to let everyone know. Assistants often make reservations for their boss and never call the travel agent to say that the trip was canceled. Airlines and hotels are becoming stricter with cancellations and now sometimes charge cancellation fees. If your boss cancels a trip, take a second and let your travel agent know.

Special Services

Some of the larger airlines have a department called Special Services that is geared toward helping celebrities and high-profile executives. Developing relationships with these people can also make your life easier. Special services can help when your boss arrives at the airport, assisting

with baggage, gate escorting, coordinating limousines, etc. I have even had special services escort a boss down the runway in a golf cart to a plane that had left the gate but had not yet taken off because they were waiting for my boss! Keep in mind that they won't do this for everyone, but I was working for the CFO (Chief Financial Officer) of a large studio in Hollywood, and he had enough clout; therefore I had enough clout!

In addition to the preferred airline, you need to know the class and type of seating that your boss likes. Some people will fly first-class on business trips and business-class on personal trips, depending on what type of travel expense their company allows them. Find out if they want window or aisle seating. This is where your special service and travel agent relationships are helpful, since they will sometimes have upgrades lying around that they can give your boss.

Ground Transportation

Getting your boss to and from the airport and meetings is an essential part of putting together a travel itinerary.

Put together a list of the number one limousine service in the cities where your boss travels the most, noting that the company you use in your home town may have sister companies in many of the major cities around the world. Then use the same service every time your boss is in that city.

This consistency will allow you to develop a good relationship with the company, and they will in turn take good care of your boss. You will be able to call them at the last minute and have everything taken care of. In turn, you will rest easier at the end of the day because you know your boss will be picked up on time—those car companies want your repeat business!

Ask your boss if she prefers town cars or limousines. Does she like to be at the airport right at the time of departure or is she the cautious type who likes to be there an hour ahead of time? Again, keep these notes handy so that you will be able to plan future trips on your own without repeating all the same questions to your boss.

As a rule, always write down the name of the person with whom you spoke when making a reservation. Also write down the date and time. These notes should be kept in your notebook for quick reference. If something goes wrong, you can call and speak with the manager and give the name of the employee and time that you spoke with them and made the arrangements. This is called CYA— "covering your ass!"

Hotels

As with airlines and transportation, make a list of your boss' hotel preferences.

Many times you will end up with a boss who travels frequently to the same city. What is her favorite hotel? Some hotels are tied into airlines and offer frequent-flier miles for staying with them. What are two backup hotels that your boss could tolerate if choice number one is booked? Does she stay in a suite on business? Does she have different preferences on personal trips? All of this information needs to go into your notes. Again, this is an opportunity for you to establish relationships that will make your life easier. The key people at hotels to send gifts to are the reservations manager and the chief concierge. They are both very helpful in making last-minute reservations and changes. They are also more likely to accommodate your employer when they are close to selling out because they know that you bring them a lot of business.

TIP FROM THE TOP: An executive assistant at Microsoft suggests being way ahead of the game with holiday travel and hotel reservations. Her computer-scheduling program reminds her a year in advance to start discussing Christmas holiday travel plans with her boss. Many of the resort hotels sell out months in advance for the Christmas season. Stay on top of your game and book a few different hotels for your boss. They can give you a few options and your boss can decide closer to his vacation which one he wants to stay at.

Corporate Rates

It does not matter how large or small your company is; every company likes to save money. Think about this fact especially when making travel plans. When making reservations with airlines, limousines, and hotels, always check if they have a special corporate rate for your company. The company accountant will take note of the savings, commend your employer, and this only makes you look that much better!

How Is Jr. Getting to Soccer Practice?

Although you may think that your vacation has started once the Big Cheese is away, tasks that are not usually your

responsibility may become your life for the duration of your employer's trip. Fido needs dog chow, the petunias need watering, and the mailbox can handle only so many catalogs. While some of you may luck into a boss who has a handy and reliable other half, many other executives are single and will need you to look after their affairs while out of town. This is a discussion that you should have with your boss while planning that first trip that you are taking such good notes on! Is she part of a weekly car pool that picks the kids up from grammar school? Does the house-keeper need to be let in? Do the cars need to be started occasionally while your boss is in the Caribbean during the winter months? There may be a whole list of little things that you will handle during your boss' absence. Again, go over these things with your employer. Remember to make it clear that you are willing to accommodate the trip, but that these are not going to become your regular responsi-bilities. You too should have a life.

Calling In

Yes, the invention of the telephone and, more specifically, the cellular telephone almost guarantees that your boss will call you from the road. You may even grow to appreciate these calls. In fact, you may have several projects at a standstill because you need her to answer some questions before you can proceed.

To be prepared for these calls, you should have the following ready in a folder:

- A phone sheet and organized messages
- Questions that need answering
- Cover sheets ready to fax the phone sheets and important paperwork
- Numbers needed to return calls with your boss on the line (also known as "conferencing in" or "rolling calls")

Finally, if your boss is going to a different time zone, ask if you need to accommodate the time difference. This simply means that if you are in L.A. and your boss is going to N.Y., does she want you to start your day three hours earlier and leave at night three hours earlier? They will be very impressed that you thought of this (gold star!). However, make it clear that you are not working double hours. If you come in earlier, you leave earlier.

Expense Reports

It is almost always the job of the executive assistant to submit expense reports for their boss' travel. Each company handles these differently and have various guidelines and forms that need to be used. Your boss will be able to direct you to the appropriate person, usually in the accounting office, who can show you the proper way to submit expense reports. You should keep a copy of all of the expense reports that you submit in a file in your office.

OK, YOU ARE GOOD TO GO, DON'T FORGET THE GUM FOR THE PLANE

A traveling boss is usually a stressed-out boss. The more organized you are and the fewer mistakes that take place during her trip, the better. If you plan well, develop good relationships, double-check every reservation that you make, and keep your computer itinerary and folder on hand and up-to-date, mistakes will be less likely to happen—which makes for a far happier boss.

TRAVEL CHEAT SHEET

Favorite Airlines:

airline	contact name	phone number	frequent flyer number
1.			
2.			
3.			
4.			

Seating preference:	window	aisle	
Personal travel:	coach	business	first class
Business travel:	coach	business	first class

Favorite Hotels Information:

name	phone number	type of room	corporate rate?
1.			
2.			
3.			
4.			
5.			
6.			

Ground Transportation: town car   limousine

Airport at: time of departure   ahead _____ minutes

company	city	contact name	phone number	account number
1.				
2.				
3.				
4.				

To use this sheet, photocopy at 141%.

CHAPTER EIGHT

Temporary Assistance

A TEMP? DAMN, I'M NOT GOING TO GET ANYTHING DONE TODAY.—Another true story from an executive assistant:

During the summer, in between my college semesters, I worked as a temporary assistant. One week I was hired to fill in for an executive assistant who worked for one of the bigger vice presidents in a large financial corporation. When the boss arrived, he exclaimed, "A temp! I never get anything done when a temp is here. Is my assistant sick? I'll just go home for the day and come back tomorrow when she is here." With that statement he turned, and started walking toward the door. "Excuse me," I said, "your assistant is on vacation for the entire week. I doubt you want to stay home for the entire week! My name is Caroline. I temp all the time and am very capable. Give me a break and try out one day with me. If, at the end of the day, it has been so horrible that you can't stand it, stay home for the remainder of the week, and I'll get paid for reading magazines!" The gentleman was shocked by my candor, but he listened to me and decided to stay for the day. By the end of the week we gave off the impression that we had worked together for years. After his assistant returned from her vacation, I received a flower arrangement and a thoughtful card from both her and her boss. From that point on, I became a regular temp in the executive offices of that company. Each new assignment at that office began with my new temporary boss saying, "You come highly recommended by my colleague."

BRINGING IN A TEMP

Every once in a while you will need to take a day off due to sickness or personal reasons. However, it's pointless to take a day off if your employer keeps calling you for everything. That is where a temp comes in.

The higher level the executive you are assisting, the more energy you need to put into choosing the person to temp for you. If your company has a human resources department, it should assist you in finding candidates. Of course it is in your best interest to interview the potential temps prior to selecting one. The temp you choose should come into the office at least one day while you are still there for a crash training course.

Make a file in your computer that clearly explains the basic functions of the office and provides pertinent information on how to get things done within your company.

Many functions you perform are above and beyond your day-to-day duties, and the temp will not need to do them. For example, he or she does not need to know many of the personal errands and favors you do for your employer. Since this person is a temporary employee in the company, they do not need to be given access to all of the confidential aspects of your employer and company.

The training day should consist of the temp shadowing you. Do not have them do anything on their own. It is important *not* to have them coping for forty-five minutes while you are doing things they should be watching and taking in. All of their energy should be focused on observing you completing your day-to-day tasks. If they follow you around for a day, they will meet everyone you come in contact with. This will give them the opportunity to observe the interaction between you and your employer and get a general feel for what their role will be during your absence. At the same time, your employer will feel more comfortable with your impending absence because she knows that she has been left in capable hands. Make sure that the temp has a notebook and is taking down the necessary notes for your office protocol. Before the temp leaves at night, you should review the day's events and answer any questions they may have. Before you allow them to leave for the day, you should feel comfortable that they are capable to take over for you during your time away.

The night before your absence, it would be a good idea to print out your information list from the computer designed for your temporary replacement. Make sure the list is up-to-date, and includes the following:

- To-do lists or daily office functions (which you have already reviewed)
- Important numbers
- The phone numbers where you can be reached (to be used only in case of emergency!)

- Names of one or two helpful office employees they can turn to if need be
- List of projects your boss is working on
- Computer passwords
- Federal Express, UPS, and messenger services account numbers
- List of important calls your boss will always take, no matter what the circumstance

They should know where your in-box is to put all of your projects, mail, etc.

All of this information should be kept in a file labeled "Temps." It should be updated regularly, and both your boss and the human resources department should know where this file is in the unfortunate event you are ill and unable to come in.

In an ideal situation, the temp you have chosen will do a great job filling your shoes and will also be liked by your boss. If this is the case, you are very lucky, and you should continue to use that temp whenever possible in your office. This practice will not only make things easier on you, but it will also make your employer feel more comfortable and more willing to give you time off. During busy periods in your office, this temp can also be used when you need additional support. It is a nice gesture to send a small gift of appreciation from you and your boss to the temp for a job well done.

TEMPORARY AGENCIES

It is in your best interest to work continuously with the same agency and the same agent. The more this person knows about you and your office, the easier it will be for them to find you good assistance. You will not always have the luxury of knowing in advance that you won't be able to go to the office on a particular day; even great assistants get sick. If you are working with a temp agency that is familiar with you and your office, they will be able to send appropriate replacements for you with little or no notice.

TIP FROM THE TOP: Chandra L. Duplantis is an account executive at Goodkind Staffing Ltd. in New York City. She suggests that companies can make their office better for temps by clearly communicating to the agency:

- What the job entails
- What skills are needed
- What the office environment is like
- What type of personality is needed

She adds that often companies choose their temp agency by looking at the different costs of different agencies. However, a smart company will choose an agency that has a more personal touch and takes the time to get to know the temps and the clients. That company will end up with the better deal because the agent is armed with the information that will allow them to find good matches. Temporary staffing is a professional line of work and should be treated as such.

CHAPTER NINE

Interns

DO YOU REALIZE THAT WHERE I AM TODAY IS DIRECTLY RELATED TO THE PROJECT YOU ARE WORKING ON? Two years ago, an intern for a very high-ranking administrative official to the president was given a task that would change his perspective on "meaningless tasks." Mind you, he was an intern on his own volition, since he did not want nor did he receive any college credit or financial compensation. He knew that working at the White House was a golden opportunity to make future contacts. The first project he was assigned to was to update the Rolodex of this well-connected and high-ranking official. He began the task thinking he was simply doing another time-consuming office chore (Oh, what can we come up with for the intern today?). The official walked into the office just as the intern had begun the data entry and number checking involved in updating a Rolodex. He asked the intern, "How's it coming with that?" The intern commented sarcastically, "Oh, I'm just havin' a party over here." The official turned his head and became quite serious. "Do you *realize* what you are doing?" he said sternly. "I'm updating your Rolodex," the intern replied. To that, the official commented, "You are not *just* updating my Rolodex. Listen, right now you are working on my lifeline. I have the job I have today because I know all of those people and they respect me." With that, he walked away, and the intern had a moment to reflect on the official's statement. This seemingly minor encounter changed the intern's viewpoint not only on that particular project, but on everything he was assigned from that point on throughout the course of his internship. He began to understand that even the seemingly smallest tasks are important and need to be done, and done well. The Rolodex he was updating was the core resource from which all of his employer's work stemmed. "I was proud to be photocopying special documents and took pride in all of my work. When you are working at the White House, everything is important, and it is an amazing feeling. You take the time to create the best experience you could ever have, as it is maybe your only opportunity there. You must make the most of any internship experience and exploit it to your advantage, whether at the White House or on Wall Street. Internships can lead to lifelong contacts and many future employment opportunities."

Establishing an internship program at your company is a great way to give something back to your community and the next generation of workers. Students get hands-on experience in their field of study. They learn responsibility. They see the "real" side of what they have been studying in books and can decide if they truly enjoy the field they have been studying. By opening your office to young students, you enable them to get one step ahead of other students by giving them contacts and experience for after graduation. It is a worthwhile cause not only for them but for you: Visualize your swamped office and the piles of work on your desk. There are never enough hours in the day to get everything done. Maybe you have suggested that your boss hire additional help. We all know how much our employers hate hiring more staff. It costs too much money. Well, the solution for you just might be interns. They usually work for school credit rather than pay, and they are generally hardworking and eager to learn. If you spend the time to carefully select the right intern for your office *and* spend the time training them properly, they can turn out to be one of your most valuable assets. Show them how to file, type memos, answer phones, and run errands, and you will notice how much extra time you have to get more work done.

HOW TO FIND THE INTERN THAT IS RIGHT FOR YOU

The best way to find an intern is through local universities and colleges. Most big schools have an internship department which will make the whole process much easier for you. Be wary of interns that are not part of a school program, since they are not accountable to anyone. There are many laws and restrictions accompanying employment without pay. It is in your company's best interest to stick with an accredited school and program, as they are used to working within the appropriate state guidelines.

Once you have decided which school you are going to work with, you will need to create a list for your intern contact at the university or college.

Use the following checklist to help organize your needs before speaking to the school.

This list is an important part of your search for an intern. Most likely, it will be posted at the school's internship office and on their e-mail job postings. The more specific and clear you are about the internship, the easier it will be for the school to weed through the applicants and find an intern that is right for you. Be very honest with yourself, since your goal is to get good office help, not impress others by having someone underfoot who runs to Starbucks every time you need a mocha.

TIP FROM THE TOP: Paula Lee is the director of the Career Services Department at New York University. She urges people who are looking for an intern to be very clear about what they need an intern for. If the job is just going to be clerical work, you need to let the school know that. On the flip side, if you are looking for someone who already has experience, you need to let the school know that as well. Paula says that sometimes people expect too much from their interns and forget that they are young, fresh college students

INTERN CHECKLIST

Job description for office intern:

_____

_____

_____

_____

Expected Hours/Duration of Internship:_____

Daily Duties:

_____

_____

_____

_____

Long-Term Projects:

1. _____
2. _____
3. _____

Required Skills:

_____

_____

_____

_____

Contact at your company who is responsible for the intern:

_____

College or University contact name and number:

_____

To use this sheet, photocopy at 141%.

who might be getting their first taste of office life. So be honest with your list of requirements, including specific computer programs and skills that you expect from your intern. The more information you can provide to the school, the more they will be able to help you with a perfect match!

THE SCHOOL COORDINATOR

A common theme that runs through this book is the idea of establishing good working relationships with people that you rely on to get your job done, i.e., the travel agent, the computer department, and the mailroom. The intern coordinator at the university or college that you have chosen to work with is no exception to this rule. Befriend this person, and your life will be easier, guaranteed! If they become familiar with you and your office, they will be able to spot potential interns for you, because they will know more about what your office needs. If you have this ally, they can be scouting out summer help for you before you've even thought about spring!

INTERVIEW THE POTENTIAL INTERNS

Once the position has been posted and the internship coordinator has done all of the necessary screening, you will be called, faxed, and approached about the coveted opening in your company. Although you are very busy, you must personally meet everyone who is interested in working with you, because phone manners, albeit very important, can be deceiving.

Do not hire an intern based on a phone call. You will
need to put aside adequate time to interview every candi-
date. Once these people walk into your office, do not size
them up by appearances alone. These possible interns are
there to impress you with their finesse, intelligence, and
ability to suit your office needs. Be prepared with intelli-
gent questions and honest answers to their questions. This
should not be fifteen minutes of social banter about what is
the latest fad at your alma mater. This is the time to find
out what skills the intern has, what skills they have that
need improvement, and what they want to get out of the
internship.

DESIGNATE AN INTERN POINT PERSON

There should be one person in your office who is designated as the intern "point person." This role is especially

important if you have more than one intern or if your interns work for more than one person in your office. The intern should report to the point person when they arrive in the morning, right after lunch, and before they leave at the end of the day. Anyone in the office who needs something done by the intern should give that assignment to the point person. This way someone is always on top of where the intern is and what the intern is doing. Your office and the intern will get more out of the internship if it is handled in this orderly fashion.

The point person will also be responsible for completing internship reports. Most schools require these reports from the company at the end of a semester. Many internships are based on a pass/fail system. These reports offer you a chance to evaluate the intern and the work that they completed over the course of their employment in your office. These reports are important to the intern and are necessary in order for the intern to pass the course. Take the time to fill it out carefully and honestly. At this point the intern has probably worked for you for a few months for free; the least you can do is give them an honest evaluation!

INTERN MANAGEMENT

It is important that you establish a system for keeping track of your intern and making the experience worthwhile for them and you. On their first day you should take them around and introduce them to everyone in the office. Have them spend their first few days shadowing you before you give them anything to do on their own. This gives them the chance to see what you do during an average day and get a feel for how the office runs. This also gives your boss an opportunity to meet the intern and start to get comfortable with having the intern around. The quicker the intern becomes part of the team, the better, especially with regards to the boss. If the boss trusts the intern, she will begin to give the intern projects, which means more time for you to get your work done.

Once the intern has shadowed you for a few days, it is time to give them a space of their own. This is essential to your sanity and theirs!

Give them a good-sized work space and stock it with all of the supplies that they will need, including an in-box where people can leave work for them to do.

If you don't give them an appropriate space of their own to work in, they will be hanging all over you and your desk all day. I promise that you will not enjoy that situation. Find them a space and let everyone in the office know where that space is.

Give the intern daily responsibilities. Teach them to prioritize a day's to-do list. In addition to their daily tasks, there will obviously be last-minute projects and memos that need to get done in a hurry. Be there to answer questions and remember to be patient. The more time that you spend helping the intern assimilate, the more they will be able to help you later on by taking work off your hands.

TIP FROM THE TOP: Paul Stark is a producer on the Ru Paul show. He has worked on many shows that employ interns, and he offers the following advice: In addition to daily tasks, give the intern a long-term project that they can work on during down time. This tactic assures that the intern isn't just sitting around waiting to get screamed at when it suddenly gets busy. When they have time to spare, they know that they can work on their project until they are needed again. It also helps them feel part of the team because they are involved in something in-depth.

KEEP THE INTERNS HAPPY

Once in a while, an intern gets blue and needs a cheer-up pep talk. We all do! Take them out for a little comfort food. You should explain to them that although filing can be a complete bore, it has to be done and it is integral to office organization. They can make the most out of it by reading or glancing over the documents that they are filing. Reading previously completed deals, memos, reports, etc., is one of the best ways to learn. If you allow them to question you on the things they have seen but do not understand, they will start paying more attention and get more excited about doing their assigned tasks. Take the time to answer their questions; just because you know who someone is or can recite a phone number off the top of your head doesn't mean everyone else can. If the intern cannot handle certain tasks, then assign them something to which they might be better suited or take a moment to explain it to them again. Do not be too quick to judge. Remember how you were when you started with a new employer. Treat the interns the same way you wanted to be treated. Do not speak condescendingly to them. If you do, they may revolt and screw up your office systems or leave you in the lurch. Not good.

Interns just want to be part of your environment, so make them feel as such. They are there to learn and soak up as much knowledge as they can in order to prepare themselves for their next internship or actual employment. Often they can greatly help you and your office by bringing in a system they learned from their previous internship or employer. Don't look down on them as "just an intern." One day you could find yourself working for them!

Internships benefit you and the intern. Take the time to make it a worthwhile experience for both of you. It's not only about running errands for Mr. Bossman and picking up the dry cleaning. It's also about young minds soaking up knowledge and, at the same time, making you look better by helping your office to run more smoothly.

CHAPTER TEN

Personal Errands and Personal Assistants

One intern at Hollywood Pictures at the Disney Studios lot in Burbank shares her first day's experience:

It was my first day. I was so excited to be working at a big movie company. I had always wanted to be in film, and this was my big break. I envisioned myself getting promoted quickly and thought a job as a producer was just around the corner. Then reality set in. I got my first assignment, I was asked to clean the office refrigerator. My heart sank. I realized that I was lowest on the totem pole. My excitement dwindled as I faced the fact that I was probably going to spend my internship doing the dirty work that no one else wanted to do. I moped into the kitchen and started taking out the old food, shelves, and general junk that had acquired over the months in the office fridge. Halfway through this humbling task I got a change of heart. I decided that I might as well make the best of it. Everyone was getting a good laugh on my behalf, so I decided not to be so down and serious and have some fun too! I cleaned that refrigerator so well that it looked like new. Throughout the course of the day, office staff of all ranks came in and out of the kitchen to get their lunch, fill up their coffee mugs, or just take a peek in the fridge to see what they could snack on. They began to comment to one another, and their conversations echoed through the halls. "Hey, who cleaned the fridge, it looks great," and "Did

we get a new refrigerator?" were the common comments that I heard. Later that day, my internship "point person" called me into his office and asked me to sit down. "You know," he said, "every semester we make the new intern clean the fridge. It is a sort of hazing ritual, but it is very telling. Most kids complain and have such a bad attitude about it, but not you. You saw the humor in it and put pride into your work as if you were working on something important. That says a lot about you. You have passed the 'good attitude' test. I am not saying that every project we're going to give you will be important, but you've proven yourself and we are now going to give you a great opportunity to work on projects that you will learn from." From then on I realized that if you have a good attitude about your work, whatever the work may be, people will notice.

PERSONAL ERRANDS

As an executive assistant, you will have to learn to handle doing your boss' personal errands. No one likes to do them, and sometimes you may feel degraded, but keep your chin up. I used to get bitter running around getting my boss' dry cleaning, washing her car, and taking her dogs to the vet. Then I looked at it from a different viewpoint—hers! She was a very busy executive at a large talent agency. She was on the phone doing business from her house as early as 7:00 A.M. She would continue making business calls from her car on her way to the office, and then switch to her office phone until lunch. At lunch, she would go to a business meeting and then come back to the office until 7:30 or 8:00. Afterward she would run off to a business dinner and get back to her house often after midnight. The next day it would start all over again. With a schedule like that, of course she had no time to do her personal errands. I was learning so much about the movie business working for her that it was a fair trade to do her errands. I knew that someday I would be successful too, and then someone could do my errands!

Many of the assistants at my talent agency had to do personal errands for their bosses. These were handled in a time-saving fashion by scheduling certain hours and days during the week to do these errands. These assistants would look at the upcoming week's schedule and pick two times that their boss was scheduled for meetings, generally during the morning hours. If the days chosen were Tuesday and Friday, they would tell their boss that those two mornings were "errand mornings." This let the boss know in advance that their assistants would be out for a few hours each of those days. Also, the boss would know to give their assistants a list of errands that needed to be done before the two scheduled days.

PERSONAL ASSISTANTS

A personal assistant is someone who knows everything about the life of their boss. Many big executives and celebrities hire a personal assistant as well as office assistants. This personal assistant knows everything about their employer, from shoe size, preferred restaurants, and car-maintenance records to their favorite laundry detergent. Generally, if you are a personal assistant, you are in charge of keeping everyone else in your boss' personal and professional domain organized and in sync. This work is often more difficult than that of an office assistant. The difference is that personal assistants conduct business from various locations (the car, vet, studio, kitchen, etc.), and an executive assistant works out of a cubicle. If you are a personal assistant, you need to discipline yourself to stay organized as if you had a regular office space.

TIP FROM THE TOP: Bonnie Kramen is the personal assistant to the well-known actress Olympia Dukakis. She keeps a pile of reading next to her bed—scripts, books, plays, you name it—all related to her work and in order of priority. It is impossible to read this kind of material at the office, so it is great to do in the quiet of the evening. She also adds, "I write down all errands and then number them in order of:

- Urgency
- Time of day (for traffic, store hours, etc.)
- Proximity

Then I bring things to do while I do errands. For example, while standing on line at the bank, I can read over a contract, a scene in a script, or edit a letter. Plan ahead to make great use of your time wherever you find yourself. You just never know when you are going to have to wait."

IF YOU WORK WITH SOMEONE WHO HAS AN EXECUTIVE OFFICE ASSISTANT

One of the keys to superstardom is to make fast friends with your boss' office assistant. Generally, you will come to depend on this person and rely on a close working relationship. You need to know all of the office appointments to enable you to coordinate your boss' personal life. You need to be in contact with this person constantly throughout the day to keep schedules coordinated. If an event occurred over the weekend to put your boss in a bad mood, you must warn your counterpart. The same goes for them if they had a bad day with the boss; you should be the first one to get a call.

IF YOU WORK ALONE

If you work solo, you are probably employed by a celebrity of some sort. Everyone from painters and socialites to actors and directors have personal assistants. There are many perks to this position. Perhaps you travel with your boss, or go to all of their charity events and meetings. The contacts you can make for the future are limitless! However, to get to the next step of your career, you must work for it. Confidentiality is essential. Your boss needs to feel able to trust you with all information and with their money.

Whether you are an executive assistant who handles personal errands or a personal assistant, you will need to be on top of the following:

- Business
- House
- Car
- Family

The Business

Even if you work for your boss outside an office, play the part of an executive assistant *in* an office. Understand the basic concepts and rules set forth in this book. Keep all business material, schedules, phone sheets, and itineraries organized. Your job will be tough because you will probably be working out of various locations.

The House

Your employer's home may be filled with responsibilities which now fall to you. Welcome to the world of alarm companies, water-delivery services, and underground sprinkler systems. This is just the beginning! If you live in the home with your boss or just house-sit occasionally, you need to take this responsibility seriously. You will have to know the number of the all-night plumber for the clogged-up sink and who to call to get the rug steamed clean before a last-minute dinner party. You should keep lists of all of the people you call, including doctors, lawyers, family members and friends, cleaning services, pool services, gardeners, painters, veterinarians, and mail sources, just to name a few. You should compile this list with your employer. You are on call twenty-four hours a day, and at all times you are the saving grace. Your boss needs to feel that he is the king of his castle and that it runs perfectly.

The Car

Keep lists of automobile(s) service records, receipts, and all service station receipts. Don't wait for the oil change reminder cards to come in the mail; you should anticipate engine checkups and already have an appointment scheduled by the time the card arrives. You can't anticipate a car emergency, so make fast friends with your boss' mechanic.

The Family

If your boss has a family, you could be working in conjunction with his or her spouse. This person can be your greatest ally or worst enemy. When hired, you should have a one-on-one conversation with this person to allow them to lay out their ground rules. Do whatever it takes to work with them and not against them. If your responsibilities include the children, make files and records for all of their doctors, immunizations, allergies, teachers, friends, and outside school activities. You wouldn't want to forget to pick up Sophie from soccer practice or Max from his piano lessons. The same thing goes for pets. Keep files on vets, immunizations, and allergies. Also, make sure the animal approves your food selection. Spot may hate the liver and onion kibbles, and would rather starve himself than eat it. It would *not* be a gold star day if you found Spot in the garden not breathing!

THE BIG PICTURE

Systems and schedules are especially important for personal assistants because they do not have the benefit of an organized office environment. Create schedules and stick to them. Have car washing on Monday, dry cleaning on Tuesday, and pool maintenance on Friday mornings. Think of ways to utilize your time as efficiently as possible. If you plan to have all house maintenance done on a certain day, you know that you must be at the house that entire day.

You can plan ahead knowing that you will have time to get through assigned reading material, catch up on the filing at the home office, make phone calls, etc. Be consistent and make your boss abide by your schedule. This will help you avoid wasted time.

TIP FROM THE TOP: David Dupuy started his career in Hollywood as a production assistant on the show *Party of Five*. He now co-owns his own production company, which has recently released its first feature film. David admits that it was hard when he was starting out at the bottom to continually motivate himself to do all of the "unimportant" jobs. He suggests that you ask as many questions as possible and learn all that you can while you are in this position. He found that people were enthusiastic to share their knowledge with the "new kid." Once he started taking the initiative and began asking questions, he found that everyone was really helpful and took him under their wing. In a way, you are in the best possible position because no one really expects much from you; you are simply running errands. Take this time with little responsibility to learn about what other people around you are doing.

As a personal assistant, you should realize that almost no task is too large or small. If your boss plans on throwing a benefit sit-down dinner for three hundred, you better get on the phone with the local hotels regarding banquet room rates. Remember, no one loves one hundred percent of their job, but the balance leans on the happy and positive! Because you are working with someone intimately, ask questions directly. It is not worth being reprimanded for assuming that your employer likes "new car scent" as opposed to "musk" at the car wash. Better to be safe and ask first rather than asking forgiveness later.

CHAPTER ELEVEN

Communication

Here's a funny little story from an executive assistant:

We had the pleasure of working with an intern named Doug (a.k.a. Intern Boy, a.k.a. I.B.). Doug was great, a little rusty on business etiquette, but the enthusiasm was there and then some! He just wanted to hang out and help. He was one of those kids who was going to an out-of-town college, but was from the local area. He knew everyone and could get anything in a moment's notice. Our boss often went from desperately needing Doug's assistance to banishing him from the office. This would happen a minimum of twenty times a day. Once, right before lunch, the boss yelled to his assistant, with Doug in earshot, "When I get back from lunch, Doug better be gone and I don't ever want to see or smell him again!" Eventually Doug just laughed at this daily ritual. Inevitably, later in the afternoon, the boss would need assistance with something suitable for Doug, and start looking around the area muttering, "Where the hell is that kid?"

Finally he'd ask his assistant, "Where's I.B.? And what has he been working on for so long that I don't know where he is? I need his help with something." And the assistant would once again inform the boss, "You fired him." Thankfully, we really never fired him because the boss would always say, "Get him back, I have something for him to work on." Usually we would just give him the afternoon off. "He'll be back in the morning," we'd tell the boss, and the next day the process of firing and rehiring Doug would start all over again.

As you can see, we figured out how to communicate with our boss, as irrational as he may have been. We knew that he was never serious about firing Doug and that he was just one of those employers who yells a lot but never really means any harm.

Communication is absolutely essential to a successful partnership between an executive and his assistant. With the amount of meetings and phone calls that takes place throughout the course of a day, there is rarely any down-time to sit around and chat about what is going on in the office. When you begin your employment in the office, you have to figure out what type of employer your boss is. Most employers fit into one of the following three categories:

THE LOU GRANT BOSS

He was there through thick and thin with Mary Tyler Moore (who was going to make it, after all!). This type of employer is fair, usually rational, easily approachable, cares about most personal issues, and maintains a democratic type of office environment. This person always publicly congratulates you for a job well done, and will speak privately to you when a project fails or is not up to par. In other words, the Lou Grant boss is not big on public humiliation and generally respects his employees and wants to see them succeed. Big congratulations on landing a position with this type of boss. It should not take you too long to be able to work well together because communication is always open and easy. Your focus can rest a hundred percent on your job. Do your job well, double-check everything, and be honest if you make a mistake. This type of boss recognizes these things and will treat you well if he thinks you are giving it your best.

THE LOUIS DIPALMA BOSS

Yes, we all remember Louis from *Taxi*. He thought every-one that worked at the Sunshine Cab Company was a

moron and never hesitated to tell them so. He was the type of employer who was out-and-out mean, irrational, completely unfair, self-serving, with a big Napoleon complex. If you do accept a position with someone with this reputation, the question I present to you is, "Why?" My second question is, "Are the rewards big enough?" If they are, then it might be worth it. For example, if this position is the only opening in a company you've always wanted to work for or the pay is extremely high and you're about to be evicted, take the job. If you have justified accepting this position for yourself, the next step is to accept the fact that effective communication will take a lot of work and, most likely, you will have to be the instigator. Do not be defensive with the Louis DiPalma–type boss, as that is a complete turnoff to this personality type. This type of boss needs all the attention, so your job is to be low-key. If you try to match their temper or yell back every time they yell at you, the office will be a nightmare and you will truly hate your job. The key to success in this position is to be extra careful and avoid mistakes. You should also document everything (fax confirmations, names and times of people that you spoke with) so that you have proof of your work when you get blamed for messing everything up. It is also essential with this employer that you understand that it is not personal! He would yell at a small child as easily as he yells at you. He has nothing against you. You just happen to be standing in front of him when he is angry.

THE JOAN CRAWFORD BOSS

Joan Crawford types are the worst bosses, because one minute you are a superstar and the next you are lower than a common housefly. Like the Louis DiPalma type, you need to have daily personal affirmation that this office is where you belong. There are ways of communicating with this person, but again, it is all going to come from you. In order to survive well and create a pleasant working environment, you must remain the consistent assistant. This means that you should not react to their mood swings. Have the same attitude no matter what their temper level. Double-check your work and be accurate. If you are a good assistant who is thorough, then you will be able to survive the good and bad moods of your boss because you will always be in the right. Treat your boss as you would if you had a Louis DiPalma boss. If you cover yourself by doing good work, they won't be able to attack you on their bad days. Do not be tempted to be pals with them when they are having their good days. You should remain a little distant at all times. Always remember, when they are in a good mood, that's the time to tell them about their mistreatment of you.

In short, beware of Dame Crawford; she can be your best friend and your worst enemy all in the course of an hour. Fear not; this relationship may work out just fine. You must simply learn that you need remain aloof and focus on the work itself.

TIP FROM THE TOP: Matt worked for several months as the assistant to Harvey Weinstein at Miramax. At first Matt was very excited, since his passion was film and he had got a job working for one of the biggest pioneers in today's film world. For various reasons, the two men's personalities clashed, and it made the working environment uncomfortable for both. Matt advises assistants to be honest with themselves about what is important to them about the job that they are doing. There will be times where a work situation or a personality clash is not reconcilable. Do not sacrifice your happiness just to work in a job that sounds good. Sometimes you have to accept that you are not in the right situation and move on.

MEETINGS

For all boss types, you can aid communication by scheduling daily, weekly, and three-month meetings.

Daily Meetings

Schedule daily meetings with your boss first thing in the morning, right after lunch, and at the end of the day. These meetings should be short and organized. They should not last more than ten or fifteen minutes. In these meetings you should review the day at hand, and discuss the next day's schedule. Also, you can update your boss on what tasks are completed or still pending, what meetings you are setting up, and the phone sheet. This may seem redundant, but because executives are so busy and things change so frequently, the three brief meetings a day schedule is essential.

Weekly Meetings

Schedule weekly meetings for late on Fridays and early on Monday mornings. The purpose of these meetings is to discuss the week's highs and lows. These meetings are much more casual than the daily meetings, and often they are for pep talks and strategizing. These may have nothing to do with the job or the work itself, but could be more about the office and the way it's running for both of you.

Three-Month Meetings (Reviews)

Set up a meeting every three months in which you will be able to get a progress report from your employer. This is the time to be especially honest with her and yourself. They will give you gold stars for some things and criticism for others. This is a session to discuss how things are working, both good and bad, and how to improve upon them. It is your job to schedule these meetings and enforce their attendance. For some reason bosses tend to avoid these meetings like the plague!

Make sure these meetings are one-on-one, when your boss is not doing other work or taking any calls. You need your boss' full attention or the meetings will not work— and they will turn out to be a waste of time for the both of you. If you implement this system and they are averse to using it, ask what would be better for them. Remember, communication goes both ways, and you need to listen to them and their ideas as well. This person probably had systems already in place before you got there, and why should they change now? It's at least as much about you adapting to their routine as them adapting to yours.

Many of you are starting out as an executive assistant in hopes of working your way up to another position within your company or field. Part of good communication involves discussing your career goals with your boss. Most of my employers asked me about my goals during my initial interview, and it was up to me to make sure that was not the last time my goals were discussed. Be open about where you want to be in a year, two years, or five years. The three-month review is the perfect time to discuss this. Let your boss know that you will give them a hundred percent of your time and efforts but that you want to move ahead too! If they don't know what you want to do with your life, how can they help you advance? Most of my former bosses have been instrumental in my career advancement by introducing me to new contacts, writing recommendations, and taking the time to teach me new things about my field. Being honest about your objectives works, try it!

These three-month reviews are also a good time to discuss vacation plans. You will not always be able to take the time off that you are requesting. If there is a certain "busy time" at your office, you may have to delay your vacation. For example, if you work for an accountant, tax season may not be the best time to plan that trip to Aruba! If you can, try to change your plans to accommodate the needs of your office. If you stay and work hard through the busy period, you may even get an extra vacation day, flowers, or dinner on the company. In most cases there will not be a problem with your vacation. Your only headache will be the frequent complaining of your boss saying, "But who the hell is filling in for you?" Make sure to set up a temp as far in advance as possible (see Chapter 8).

COMMUNICATING WITH THE TEAM

TIP FROM THE TOP: Nancy Nemecek worked as an assistant to Michael Eisner. At the time of her employment, Mr. Eisner had seven assistants. Nancy says that when there is more than one assistant, it is very important to learn to work together as a group. Competition among the group would be disastrous to productivity.

If you work in an office that has several staff members, good communication with them is as important as good communication with your boss. Schedule one meeting on Monday morning and one meeting Friday afternoon with the entire staff. Use this time to update each other on new projects and progress that has been made during the week on current projects. This is a good time to get and offer help. If your department is swamped with deadlines, ask some of the staff with a less hectic week to help out. On the flip side, if you are having a slow week, offer to help out in other areas.

TIP FROM THE TOP: At Bragman, Nyman, Cafarelli, a major Los Angeles publicity firm, the staff members keep each other updated by using their in-house e-mail system. If someone needs help with something or just needs to update colleagues on a particular project, they send a "flash" e-mail. This way everyone in the company is in sync, and they also save paper by avoiding unnecessary memos.

EARNING TRUST

Central to all good relationships is the concept of trust. Trust is built on good communication and honesty. If you earn your boss' and colleagues' trust, they will give you more freedom—they will know that they are in capable hands. An important factor in earning trust is how you choose to handle mistakes. If you make a mistake, own up to it. Do not try to cover it up. Buried mistakes only grow or come back to haunt you. No one wants to hear your excuses—admit your error, apologize, and make the correction.

TIP FROM THE TOP: Renee Rosen, an executive assistant at Universal Pictures, advises being honest with your boss, especially when you have made a mistake. Rather than hide the mistake and wait for the inevitable—being caught— Renee suggests that you tell your boss immediately. Go into her office and say: "I am sorry, I made a mistake, what can I do to fix it?" Your employer will appreciate your honesty, and nine times out of ten there is a way to fix the mistake. This will help build trust between you and your boss.

CHAPTER TWELVE

The Dress Code

NO, MY APARTMENT IS NOT DARK IN THE MORNING. . . .
In an effort to get to work quickly, we sometimes pay less
attention than we should to our style of dress. The following
is a true story from an assistant:

It was crunch time at the office for our projects. Either the
projects were going to fly or they were not. Presentations
had to be a hundred percent perfect and on the boss' desk
the night before he asked for them! Everyone was working
fourteen-hour (plus) days. On one of these mornings I was
due at the office extra early; of course, I woke up late that
particular morning! I threw on something I had worn just a
few days earlier, grabbed some shoes, and flew out the
door. The morning was crazy. It was not until lunchtime that I
finally sat down at my desk. I threw my feet up on the desk
and closed my eyes. I was startled by shrieks of laughter
from behind me. Imagine my horror when I opened my eyes
and discovered the source of the hysterics. In my rush to get

out the door that morning, I had picked up the wrong shoes. Each shoe was a different color and heel size. I had been so tired and crazed, I hadn't noticed all morning. I chalked my mistake to my dedication to my office responsibilities!

Your first day at a new job creates quite an impression on your new co-workers. It is true, as they say, "You never have a second chance to make a first impression." Pay attention to the dress code of the office at your initial interview. That way, on your first day, you will know how to "blend" in. While fashion can be a way of stating one's personality, the office is not the proper forum.

We all make mistakes, especially when it comes to office fashion. If you need help, buy some current trendy magazines. These magazines usually have articles called "How to Look Great for Under $500" and "Ten Clothing Items You Can't Live Without."

I am not a fashion expert, but I put together a few basic rules to supplement your magazine research:

DOS

- Simple is best
- Own at least one black suit.
- Buy solid-colored shirts and pants.
- The iron is your friend. The wrinkled look is early eighties.
- When unsure of what color stocking to wear, chose nude or the closest to your skin tone.
- Always wear socks or stockings with pants.
- Buy items that are your size! Don't try to hide in your clothing. It looks sloppy.
- There is a difference between day and evening wear. If you intend to go out at night directly from the office, bring a change of clothes. Rhinestones are not intended for daylight hours.
- If you are vertically challenged (short), invest in a pair of boots to give you a little height and presence.
- Your hair should be neat and tidy! If you have long or unruly hair, it should be pulled back with a nice clip or barrette.
- Office makeup and evening makeup should not look the same. Minimal makeup in neutral tones is best for the office.

- Always wear an undershirt when wearing a white or thin dress shirt. If you can see through it, so can everyone else.

DON'TS

- Do not wrap sweaters or shirts around your waist. Wear it properly or don't wear it at all.
- Unless you are trying to look like a cheerleader, do not wear thigh-high stockings or socks with a short skirt or dress.
- Fringe? Ah, no.
- Half shirts? No!
- Sandals? No.

- If you accessorize, do not blind others with huge hoop earrings, bracelets, and belts.
- Just because a sundress is a "dress" does not mean it is an office item. Keep string halter tops and dresses for weekend wear.
- Save the sweat suits or workout ensembles for the weekend.
- Test your clothes. In your new skirt, ask yourself, "Can I pick up that rubber band from the floor without my bloomers showing?" You may think the length is okay, but your boss probably won't.
- Don't take your shoes off in the office, even at your desk.
- If you go to the health club during lunch, make sure there are shower facilities available and *use them*! Just changing your clothes and applying a little deodorant will not do.
- Casual day does not mean pajama day. Try tailored trousers or skirt and a shirt. If you wear jeans, make sure they are not overly baggy or ripped.
- Try not to "out-dress" your boss.

TIP FROM THE TOP: Matthew Moneypenny worked for several years in the marketing department of Ralph Lauren. He adds the following helpful dressing tips:

- If you want to be treated as a professional, you should dress like a professional. For example, if your office offers casual day, you should still come to work wearing a tie. This gives the impression that you view Friday as the last day of the workweek, not the first day of the weekend. Try to see how the upper levels of management react to casual day. You will find that most executives still look like the executives they have worked so hard to become.

- A well-pressed twenty-five-dollar Gap shirt gives a better impression than a two-hundred-dollar wrinkled Armani. In addition to pressing your work clothes, take the time to have pants, skirts, and suit jackets tailored. Basic tailoring is inexpensive and gives a more refined look.

- It is a better strategy to invest in pieces from The Gap, Brooks Brothers, Banana Republic, and J. Crew than trying to buy a couple of designer pieces that will look dated after a couple of seasons (and probably not hold up to the rigors of life as an assistant).

- Build your wardrobe from basic pieces. For men, buy a couple of pairs of dark wool dress pants. Navy and gray don't show stains and work with virtually all shirt and tie combinations. Cotton khakis make you look like you are still in school, and black pants of any material will make you look like a waiter. Shirts should be solid whites or solid shades of blue. If you have to have a pattern, buy conservative stripes or plaids in grays, blue, or white.

- Women should invest in similar pieces. Suits should be navy, gray, or black. Do not wear anything to work that you might wear on a date (tight tops, open-toed shoes, spaghetti straps, extremely high heels, big jewelry, etc.)

- Try to avoid haircuts that require lots of maintenance. You will be spending unforgivable hours at your office, and every minute you spend getting ready is one you could have spent in bed. Also, bad hair days seem to be more common with people who use considerable amounts of mousse, gel, or hair spray. Feeling self-conscious because you don't feel you look your best will take away from your focus at work. Keep it simple and spend your energy on something other than brushing and blow-drying. Hint: Any hairstyle that requires a diffuser should be reconsidered!

- Women, take it easy with the makeup. Never wear a color that you would not find naturally on your body! Try to enhance your appearance with cosmetics as opposed to altering it.

In short, keep it simple, classy, and neat. Buy some magazines or spend a day with that friend of yours who always "looks perfect." Keep your work clothes separate from your play clothes. Take good care of these clothes (that means, spend the money on a good dry-cleaning service.) "Taste" is not for sale, and you do not have to be a millionaire to look good.

CHAPTER THIRTEEN

The Cheat Book

The Cheat Book is a three-ring binder with various lists of information that are vital throughout the course of each day. The advantages of this book are numerous. First, it is faster than using your Rolodex (even faster than the computerized system). Second, you can bring it home with you when you leave the office. Third, if an intern needs to call the doctor for your employer because you dashed over to make a quick copy, they can grab the cheat book and get the number. Fourth, it will be much easier for a temp to assimilate into the office.

You should make two cheat books, one on your desk and one in your boss' office.

The cheat book should contain the following information:

- a client or business associate list
- a list of all of the your employer's family members
- all of your employer's friends
- your boss's personal emergency numbers, including

doctors, lawyers, travel agent, florist, housekeepers, handyman, driver's license number, Social Security number, passport, bank account, and charge card numbers

- if applicable, any numbers relevant to your employer's children, i.e., teachers, soccer coaches, archery instructor, what have you . . .
- if applicable, inter-office extension listing
- lawyers for business associates and clientele base
- restaurant list (we suggest all of the area's restaurants *and* the separate list of all of the restaurants your employer prefers)
- list of current projects your employer is working on (not your list)

You may want to use a protective sheet or laminate these pages for your book. They will wear and tear fast because you will flip through them often.

All of these lists should be complete with all relevant information, including phone and fax numbers, addresses and perhaps birthdays of clients and/or business associates.

TIP FROM THE TOP: Bonnie Kramen, personal assistant to Olympia Dukakis, adds, "Be sure to have charge card numbers, driver's license numbers, doctors' numbers, Social Security numbers of all key people, and bank account numbers—I can't count the times these items have come in handy on the road, especially when they get lost. Ever try to get a passport overnight?"

Keep in mind that often a lot of the information within these books is not for public consumption. Therefore, your cheat book should not be left out for just anyone to glance through. You, your boss, and your intern should know where the two books are at all times. It will be up to your boss if he wants temps to have access to this book.

Closing Words

Congratulations!

You are now equipped with the tools necessary to organize yourself, your office and your boss. I have given you the basics, now it is up to you to take the next step and develop your own systems. Use the information that you have learned from this book, adapt it, and expand on it to suit the needs of your particular office environment.

Every so often, you can skim through the book for a quick refresher course! I have been working for many years, but still find it useful to brush up my organizing skills.

The most important tool you can have in the office is a good attitude. If you take pride in your work, others will notice, especially your boss. So take these tips and advice to heart and get to it. They have worked well for me and I hope they will do the same for you.

Index

Airlines, 83–84
Anger, 3–4

Burton, Sarah, 10–11, 71
Business associates, 2–3
Business errands, 116–17

Car errands, 117
Cheat Book, 141–43
Clients, 2–3
  files for, 60
Communication, 121–31
  earning trust, 130
  Joan Crawford boss,
    125–26
  Lou Grant boss, 123
  Louis DePalma boss,
    123–25
  meetings, 126–29
  with the team, 129–30

Computers, 46–63
  backing up, 57
  boss file, 60–61
  client files, 60
  E-mail, 55–56
  Internet, 56–57
  know your computer,
    49–59
  meeting the computer
    geeks, 47–49
  office files, 60
  organizing your desktop,
    59–61
  phone sheet, 23, 26
  rebooting, 57–58
  resources, 61–63
  Rolodex programs, 31
  software, *see* Software
  updating, 58
  your file, 61

Confidentiality, 6
Conflicts, 3–4
Cubicles and surrounding
    office area, 4–5

Dress code, 133–39
  don'ts, 136–39
  dos, 135–36
Dukakis, Olympia, 115, 142
Duplantis, Chandra L., 98
Dupuy, David, 119

Eisner, Michael, 36, 129
E-mail, 55–56
Expense reports, travel,
    89–90

Family errands, 118
Federal Express, 33–34
Files/filing, 39–45
  boss, 41, 60–61
  client, 60
  filers, 44–45
  follow-up, 43
  general, 41, 60
  record of, 43
  storage, 43–44
  temporary, 42
  transitional, 42
  travel, 78–79
  your, 41–42, 61
Fishbaugh, Marsha, 6, 22

Friendship, 5
FYI (For Your Information),
    28–29

Gossip, 6
Grudges, 4
Gunther, Craig, 63

House errands, 117

Important number card,
    31–32
Internet, 56–57
Interns, 99–109
  best way to find, 101–102
  checklist for, 103
  interviewing potential,
    104–105
  keeping them happy,
    108–109
  management of, 106–107
  point person for, 105–106
  school coordinators for,
    104
Itineraries, 79–82

Johnson, Jim, 17

Kramen, Bonnie, 115, 142

Lee, Paula, 102
Log books, 25, 27, 28

Mail, 33–38
  components of, 35
  mailroom, 37–38
  personal and confidential,
    36–37
  tracking, 35–36
Meetings, 65–75
  cheat sheet, 75
  communication and, 126–29
  daily, 127
  escape scenarios, 74
  setting up, 67–71
    agendas, 70
    confirmations, 69–70
    location, date, and time,
      68–69
    participants, 67–68
  three-month (reviews),
    127–29
  weekly, 127
  see also Schedules
Message pads, 25, 27, 28
Miller, Dan, 48
Moneypenny, Matthew, 137
Murphy, Larry, 44

Nemecek, Nancy, 36, 129
North, Oliver L., 6, 22

Office etiquette, 1–8
  business associates, 2–3
  clients, 2–3

  conflicts, 3–4
  cubicle and surrounding
    office area, 4–5
  gossip, 6
  making friends, 5
  questions, 7
  random tidbits, 8
  time, 7

Paperwork, *see* Files/filing
Personal assistants, 114–15
  big picture, 119–20
  working with, 115–16
Personal electronic organizers, 31
Personal errands, 111–14
  business, 116–17
  car, 117
  family, 118
  good attitude and, 111–13
  house, 117
  travel arrangements and,
    87–88

Questions, 7

Reviews, employment,
  127–29
Rolodexing phone calls,
  29–31
Rolodex software program,
  52–53

Rolston, Matthew, 17
Rosen, Renee, 45, 73, 131

Schedules:
  maintaining organized,
    71–72
  personal, 73–74
  restaurant/location list,
    72–73
Snider, Stacey, 45, 73
Software, 50–56
  accounting, 53–54
  advanced, 53
  E-mail, 55–56
  intermediate, 52
  paint/draw, 54–55
  Rolodex, 52–53
  spreadsheet, 50–51
  word processing, 50–51
Stark, Paul, 107

Tattletales, 4
Telephones, 9–32
  etiquette, 9–17
    sheet, 12–16
  FYI, 28–29
  important number card,
    31–32
  listening in on calls, 18–21
  message pads and log
    books, 25, 27, 28

phone system, 17–18
  cheat sheet, 19
  Rolodexing calls, 29–31
  tracking calls, 21–25
  telephone sheet for, 22–25,
    26
Temporary assistance, 93–98
  agencies specializing in,
    98
  bringing in, 95–97
Time, 7
Travel, 77–91
  agents/in-house services, 83
  airlines, 83–84
  calling in, 89
  cheat sheet, 91
  corporate rates, 87
  expense reports, 89–90
  file, 78–79
  ground transportation,
    85–86
  hotels, 86–87
  itineraries, 79–82
  personal arrangements,
    87–88
  special services, 84–85
Trust, earning, 130

Wantland, Danny, 37
Weinstein, Harvey, 126
Whitesman, Deena, 83